Praise for *Our Planet Powered by AI*

"The biggest challenge facing humanity is that the entropy in our global ecosystem in rising. History has proven that every ancient civilization reached a pinnacle and then self-destructed. The Greeks did it. The Romans did it. The Mesopotamians did it. Are we not approaching a similar point in our global civilization today? Consider the nuclear threats, the regional conflicts, the worldwide pandemics, and, above all, the global environmental deterioration. Technology is the only systemic fix for these growing challenges that the world is facing. Mark's research and treatise on *Our Planet Powered by AI* offer the cure for such endemic issues that plague the world today.

"In our everyday life, we continue to be shackled by daily chores. Humankind's creativity has been held hostage by its needs for sustenance. AI will be the ultimate liberator, which will free humans from worrying about daily chores and basic needs, and allow them to leverage their creative thinking to create a better world. There is no greater champion for such AI-fostered improved human experiences than Mark Minevich."

—Chetan Dube, president and
CEO of Amelia, an IPsoft Company

"Mark Minevich is on the forefront of AI in fashion and his knowledge will be both fundamental and transformative as we enter this new world."

—Morgan Romano, Miss USA 2022

"Mark Minevich's vision laid out in *Our Planet Powered by AI* is what the world needs at this crucial moment in our history. The time for us to act is now: to set up the human race for success and progress in the decades to come. Read Mark's words and heed his advice."

—Dr. Frank-Jürgen Richter,
chairman of HORASIS

"Mark Minevich's *Our Planet Powered by AI* presents a vital vision that the world requires at this pivotal moment in our time line. It is imperative that we take action immediately to prepare humanity for success and advancement in the years ahead."

—Dr. Kira Radinsky, CEO and
co-founder at Diagnostic Robotics

"*Our Planet Powered by AI* is a pivotal guide for harnessing AI's potential for a sustainable future. A must-read for leaders and innovators in every sector."

—Professor Roman V. Yampolskiy, author of
Artificial Superintelligence: A Futuristic Approach

"I have seen firsthand in my work and travels the great things that artificial intelligence can do for the human race: from helping us create more sustainable energy, to bettering our direction in climate change, to things as crucial as creating breathable air and drinkable water for those in need. In *Our Planet Powered by AI* Mark Minevich shows us the way to a better future, by harnessing AI to power positive change and create a better direction for our world."
—Irakli Beridze, head of the Centre for Artificial Intelligence and Robotics at UNICRI, United Nations

"AI plays an enormous role in shaping our lives and civilization. In his new book, Mark Minevich explains, frames, and drives the global conversation about AI and digital transformation. An inspiring read for anyone interested in the intersection of humanity and technology."
—François Candelon, Global Director, BCG Henderson Institute

"Loved how this insights-packed book proposes a transformative paradigm in deploying AI for the planet: not as a tool to mitigate damage, but as a way to leverage data and knowledge to change how we produce, consume, and live."
—Dr. Marielza Oliveira, UNESCO Director for Partnerships and Operational Programme Monitoring, Communications and Information Sector

"Thought-provoking and imperative, Mark outlines the importance of this evolving space and how we as a society need to give considerable thought to its applications and implications as both an amplifier and accelerator to our workforce, and the burden of ethics and morality behind such evolutions. It is a must read!"
—Sol Rashidi, Top 10 Women in Data & Applied; former CDO Royal Caribbean, Sony Music, Merck; CAO of Estée Lauder

In this book, Mark shares his intriguing life journey from Ukraine to a pillar of the technology community the US and the world, how his fascination as a kid grew to a life mission of how technology can be applied to empower and improve our world. Mark's has had a tremendous impact in the world through his through leadership and inspiration - and this book could not be more timely or more important - Artificial Intelligence is bringing some some of the biggest opportunities for our society - as much as the opportunities can not be ignored and risks can not, and Mark is sharing frameworks of how humanity can navigate this opportunity and mitigate the risks.
—Nicolai Wadstrom, Founder, CEO and General Partner, BootstrapLabs

"A must-read for anyone interested in the intersection of AI, sustainability, and responsible leadership, *Our Planet Powered by AI* is a valuable addition to the field."
—Elizabeth Adams, award-winning leader of Responsible AI; LinkedIn Top Voice; Affiliate Fellow, Stanford Institute for Human-Centered Artificial Intelligence

OUR PLANET POWERED BY AI

How We Use Artificial Intelligence
to Create a Sustainable Future for Humanity

MARK MINEVICH

WILEY

Published by John Wiley & Sons, Inc., Hoboken, New Jersey.
Published simultaneously in Canada.

For general information on our other products and services or for technical support, please contact our Customer Care Department within the United States at (800) 762-2974, outside the United States at (317) 572-3993 or fax (317) 572-4002.

Wiley also publishes its books in a variety of electronic formats. Some content that appears in print may not be available in electronic formats. For more information about Wiley products, visit our web site at www.wiley.com.

Library of Congress Cataloging-in-Publication Data:

Names: Minevich, Mark, author.
Title: Our planet powered by AI: how we use artificial intelligence to
   create a sustainable future for humanity / Mark Minevich.
Description: Hoboken, New Jersey: John Wiley & Sons, Inc., [2024] |
   Includes bibliographical references and index.
Identifiers: LCCN 2023025318 (print) | LCCN 2023025319 (ebook) | ISBN
   9781394180608 (hardback) | ISBN 9781394180745 (adobe pdf) | ISBN
   9781394180615 (epub)
Subjects: LCSH: Sustainable development—Technological innovations. |
   Artificial intelligence—Environmental aspects. | Artificial
   intelligence—Industrial applications.
Classification: LCC HC79.E5 M5344 2024 (print) | LCC HC79.E5 (ebook) |
   DDC 338.9/27—dc23/eng/20230721
LC record available at https://lccn.loc.gov/2023025318
LC ebook record available at https://lccn.loc.gov/2023025319

Cover Design: Wiley
Cover Image: © Vit-Mar/Shutterstock
Author Image: Courtesy of the Author

SKY10054557_090523

I dedicate this book to two remarkable people who have left a lasting impact on my life—my dear mother, Golda and my mother-in-law, Rakhil. Unfortunately, they each passed away, in March 2023 and August 2022, respectively. By dedicating this book to them, I hope to keep their memories alive in the hearts and minds of people all over the world. I will always love and remember them.

Golda and Rakhil embodied resilience, determination, and the American dream. Winning isn't about never failing, but about never giving up. Their aspirations have the power to inspire the next generation and reignite the American spirit.

Rakhil showed us the key to a well-lived life, the necessities for living well, without which life is not fulfilling. Golda was an extraordinary woman and a survivor of the Holocaust who witnessed both the best and worst of humanity in her lifetime. Despite all of her struggles, she managed to keep her priorities straight, reminding us of what truly matters in life.

It's easy to become sidetracked by trivial matters and lose sight of what's important. Nevertheless, we should focus on the things that truly matter. Golda and Rakhil's legacy is one of great beauty and should be remembered always. Although they're gone, they'll forever live on in our hearts.

Contents

Foreword

Never before has the phrase "the future is now" been more apropos. Fast-evolving digital technologies and exhilarating advancements in artificial intelligence are transforming every aspect of human life at what seems to be supersonic speed. We are in the midst of an exhilarating revolution, the likes of which we have never seen, and it's clear that extraordinary times of change and innovation demand from us extreme unbridled humanity, to ensure that these pioneering technologies enhance human life and not overtake us.

Few grasp the gravity of this essential duality more than Mark Minevich—a brilliant wizard mind in the trailblazing sphere of digitization and artificial intelligence, whose mastery of ever-advancing technologies is matched only by his deep reverence for humanity. The bridging of the two—science and soul—at this critical juncture in our world's evolution is clearly what sets Minevich apart from others in this transformative era. This renowned AI strategist and pioneer's *Our Planet powered by AI* not only delivers an exciting and practical discussion of how to implement groundbreaking artificial intelligence technologies at every level of your organization, but it also offers the most visionary, conscious, and compassionate strategies to ensure that the application of these innovations are used to create a more sustainable, equitable, and just world for all.

This is what drives Mark Minevich, and what sets him apart.

He is clearly a man on a mission, driven to combine and converge social innovation and impact with the exciting and fast-evolving worlds of digitization and artificial intelligence. His mind in this space is unparalleled, but his heart and reverence for humans is perhaps what fuels a deep calling to enhance lives by making this new world of advancing paradigms accessible to all.

In his writings, you will learn to create sustainable effective competitive advantage by introducing previously unheard-of levels of adaptability, resilience, and innovation into your company. But, just as essential, Mark sees these groundbreaking innovations as opportunities to truly optimize the human experience and views progress not just through profits and wealth building, but also in how these new efficiencies can be applied to truly empower our lives, help us solve our most pressing problems, address critical issues threatening the planet like climate change, health care, the environment, access to capital, systemic inequities, the military, and even how we navigate a shifting and tumultuous world order.

Addressing the vital concerns facing humanity matters to Mark, perhaps more than most. He came from humble beginnings, the son of immigrants, born in Ukraine, former Soviet Union—persecuted as Jews, forced to flee his homeland. His blessed mother, who recently passed away, betrayed by a broken health care system, was a Holocaust survivor, who taught him to never give up. When he came to the States, it was not easy, but newfound freedom and opportunity would define a new way forward with the hope and promise of a better future. A love of all things technology would become his passion and for his gifted mind, a natural fit that would propel his way forward into the highest stratosphere of his field. Mark has made clear that his traumatic childhood, experiencing firsthand man's inhumanity to man, has framed a lens on life that drives his vision for a more just future.

As every corner of the globe races for supremacy in the world of AI and digital domination, Mark knows all too well the perils of such innovation, especially in the wrong hands. He is sounding the clarion call for ethicists, social scientists, humanists, and philosophers to engage in the development of AI so it is aligned to human values, including morality.

We are already seeing the danger of online deep fake images of world leaders or AI chatbots that give advice on criminal activities, bad actors using the technology to spread misinformation and clone our voices. Some believe AI could pose an existential threat to humanity. There have been calls to put the technology on hold to review and reassess the potential risks of the technology.

Mark rejects that suppression, as other countries are already integrating technologies into their systems, and those who advance will dominate the world. The genie is out of the bottle he says, and the way forward is not to stop it, but to harness its power consciously, ethically, and responsibly.

When he speaks on these critical matters, bridging science and soul, the world listens. Its applications are riveting and the potential is as exciting as it gets. Mark is passionate about the opportunities that come with such groundbreaking technologies. As the foremost authority in AI and the field of digitization, the demand for his decisive expertise has him traverse every corner of the globe. He has been featured as a celebrated speaker at Davos, the United Nations, the G20, advising heads of nations, royalty, and titans of industry, with whom he shares visionary strategies on how companies can integrate AI and digitalization to hyperenhance business models, competitive edge, productivity, and performance at all levels of their organizations.

Using real-world case studies from a variety of well-known industry and business leaders Mark explains the strategic archetypes, technological infrastructures, and cultures of sustainability you'll need to ensure that your firm's next-level digital transformation takes root. You'll also discover how AI can enable new business strategies, models, and ecosystems of innovation and growth.

You will learn what it means to enable all-inclusive artificial intelligence—an engaging and hands-on exploration of how to take your firm to new levels of dynamism and growth, *One Sustainable Planet Powered by AI* will earn a place in the libraries of managers, executives, directors, and other business and technology leaders seeking to distinguish their companies in a new age of astonishing technological advancement and fierce competition.

Mark is just as passionate, if not more, about the good AI and digitization can do for the planet, for people, for the human race. We human beings are at a definitive crossroads, and no one is more adept than Mark at humanizing these advancing technologies in the most sustainable, just, and equitable ways.

I recently had lunch with Mark and his beautiful wife and daughter. We spoke of political divides across the globe and here at home, and how these advancing technologies could be used to enhance the human race or destroy it. Stories of his travels to Saudi Arabia, Brazil, Japan, Switzerland,

and beyond widened my lens on how these advancements are already changing the world and opened windows in my mind on the exciting possible applications to come, if in the right hands. We also spoke of the very real dangers and terror ahead if we forgo our reverence for humanity and allow the technologies to overtake us.

I met Mark through a dear friend when my entire online life was hacked by cyber intruders. As busy as he is, he devoted himself to helping to resolve my cyber issues. I mention this because he's a busy guy and didn't have to do it. But he did. And that tells you everything you need to know. He's a humanist with unparalleled mastery of the newest, most exciting technologies the world has ever known, and he took time to help a friend.

As I prepared to leave that lunch and the most dynamic and stimulating discussion on AI and digital advancements, I felt awe for his brilliant mind but even more so for his huge heart and mission to harness the advancements for good. Several times I caught him gazing at his young daughter.

And that, I realized, is what drives him most. Mark Minevich is intent on harnessing the power of technology to ensure a better life, not only for his daughter but for all our children. What you are about to read will give you the blueprint on how to do just that. This is your guidepost for the future from one of the most brilliant minds and biggest hearts in the field.

Prepare to be in awe.

—Giselle Fernández, seven-time Emmy Award–winning television
journalist, producer, news anchor, and philanthropist

Introduction

First, thank you for taking time from what I'm sure is a busy day, week, month, year, and full life to read what I have written. I decided to write *One Sustainable Planet Powered by AI* because I felt it needed to be written. As a people, the human race, we are at a crossroads, a nexus. We all have what feels like the entire world coming at us, all at once, every day—through our televisions, our computers, and our smartphones.

This can make it hard for any one of us to zoom out and see the entire theater of the world. The constant messaging makes it difficult to see how all of these things work together, work against each other, work against us, and, at times, work for us. That is where this book will focus—how we can all zoom out and untangle this mess and make the world work for the betterment of humanity.

What This Book Contains

Throughout the coming chapters you will read about the current state of the world, how we got where we are, my vision of how we move forward, and the thoughts of other visionaries in the world of artificial intelligence (AI) and digitization.

I will go through the movement from the 2010s to the current day of companies that have integrated AI and digitalization extensively throughout their organization, subsequently experiencing stock prices averaging four times the performance of the S&P 500. Drawing on my experience and expertise, I will show how enterprises can transform using sustainable models with societal impact.

I will provide insights and trends from leading companies, and thoroughly explain what it means to be fueled by sustainable and human-centric AI, from strategic archetypes for adoption to the necessary technological infrastructure.

But it's not only big companies or tech companies, the Googles and Amazons of the world, that can benefit from sustainable and human-centric AI. Small to midsize companies, including legacy businesses, can benefit by fully embracing and integrating sustainable and human-centric AI and digital transformation into their business practices and strategies.

I will give you the fundamentals of what it means to install all-inclusive AI to transform your business and beat out the competition to drive your businesses and the world to a better place. And I will show how a company's leadership and sustainable culture is fundamental to a thriving human-centric AI-powered transformation.

You will learn the ways AI can enable new business strategies, models, and ecosystems for innovation and growth with social/societal impact, and, finally, how to create societal benefits, social impact, and ethical AI capabilities through transparency, fairness, reliability, privacy, safety, robustness, and more.

But before we get to all that, I want to truly introduce myself to you. I want to tell you why I am writing this book, what this vision means to me, and what the world I want to help build for my daughter looks like. First, I want to tell you about the amazing people who brought me into this world, raised me, and instilled in me my work ethic, passion, and drive that I draw on to this very day.

From Eastern Europe to the United States

My life began in the Union of Soviet Socialists and Republics, in a region presently called Ukraine. Politics, wars, strife, and struggle have plagued my homeland since before my time until this very day.

I was born and grew up in the city of Lviv. Lviv went through a lot of changes over many years. It was occupied by Nazis and Germans, it was once part of Poland in the Austro-Hungarian Empire, and it was part of

Romania at one point. But at the time I was born in Lviv, it was one of the most western cities in the former Soviet Union.

My Parents' Background

The challenges that faced my family were heartbreaking and unforgivable. My grandfather was jailed, accused of attending forbidden religious events and participating in activities against the Soviet regime. We were discriminated against for being Jewish and were isolated.

During my childhood we didn't have much wealth—no one did. We relied on my dad's ability to make a living and work to provide for us. But because of the circumstances and lack of possibilities, my dad never had a chance to complete his education. His mother died very, very young during or toward the end of World War II, when his family was living in exile in Uzbekistan.

When Dad was 13 years old, he had to drop out of school to support his sisters and work in the fields. One of the skills that he learned was to become a mechanic, and later he became a mechanic of sewing machines to support us.

My mother was a Holocaust survivor. She, along with several of her family members in concentration camps, barely survived. My resolve and determination comes from my parents. I can never give up, because it would be a failure of everything they instilled in me and stood for. Sadly, my incredible mother passed away in New Jersey due to a hospital-induced infection in March 2023 as I was writing this book.

In all, we were an average family in Ukraine at the time. We didn't have much means whatsoever, living under the oppressive Soviet regime; the president at that time was Leonid Brezhnev, the head of the Communist Party. It was a difficult time; I remember that you couldn't get supplies, and the waiting lines were very long.

Leaving Ukraine

We also had to live with the secret police, and people would pick on me, especially those from minorities or different religions in school. It was a difficult childhood, and so my mom and dad made a decision: they decided that they were going to leave the Soviet Union. They were going to renounce their regime.

Of course, to leave, you had to quit your job and leave a lot of your belongings and assets, and in the end, you didn't know where you were going. Fortunately, we had relatives in the United States. My mom had a sister who had immigrated earlier and lived in New Jersey, and my dad had a sister who lived in New York, so we started on a journey to be reunited with them.

It was not a fairytale from there. I was just a little boy, nine or so years old. We had a lot of challenges. We were struggling, trying to free our minds and spirits from the Soviet dictatorship and regime, and we were looking for something better—a better life, a better opportunity for me and my brother, and hopefully a college education that would allow us to have a shot at the world.

Even knowing that we would have a lot of challenges moving to a faraway country where we didn't speak the language, the option of staying in the former Soviet Union and under the Soviet regime was far worse than taking a chance and leaving. We filed all the paperwork and received permission from the United States to travel. We also were able to get permission from the Soviets to leave the country, but it took years to get it.

Obviously, denounce the regime meant that we were going to leave our assets, we were not going to communicate with our Ukraine-based relatives, we would never come back, and we would never have citizenship again. It was a one-way ticket the regime was happy to use to push us out.

My memories of that time are brutal, but my parents made a decision to improve all our lives. They believed that opportunities would be significantly better in the United States.

Joining the United States

The journey to the United States wasn't easy. We passed through several European countries such as Austria, the Czech Republic, Italy, and others. We spent months traveling, but finally arrived in the United States as legal immigrants.

Today I can still clearly remember the first week we arrived in the United States. We were settled into a home for not more than a few days when we were robbed at gunpoint. Not such a great welcome to the United States!

To support our family, my dad had to work numerous jobs, sometimes three or four. We didn't get the chance to see him much. He took on a lot of responsibility and felt that he had to really work hard so that he could sustain us and our life in the United States. Needless to say, I always felt like I needed to repay my dad for all that he did for us, as well as my mom, for all the care and nurturing she gave us.

Because we got to take advantage of the opportunity of being in this amazing country that is the United States, as a child, I started thinking about the potential of what we could do and what could happen in the future. I knew that my dad would continue to work hard to support us, but it was always on my mind that the future and what would happen would depend on me and my generation and what we made of it.

I believe that going through all those challenges created a need in me to do something special in life. I want to create opportunities, from a societal perspective, so that not only we, but other families and people as well, will be helped in the process.

I can say that today, and with all the experiences from my childhood, I'm very proud that I have an ability to see the world through a slightly different lens and to have a unique perspective.

Where My Love of Science and Technology Was Born

When early personal computers came out, I was immediately intrigued. The first Commodore 64 came out when I was a teenager in the early 1980s. I kept thinking "What is this computer system?" It was my first "aha!" moment, and I remember sitting in school, and at home, and going to the library and constantly thinking, "What are those systems?"

I knew that as humans we had an amazing ability to memorize things, but suddenly computer systems were coming and you could store information and store documents! At that time there were visual BASIC applications that were very primitive, but we started to be able to do some basic programming on the computer. You could calculate things quickly, and you could type things quickly and print them out! It was, and still is, amazing to me.

My Other "Aha!" Moments

Later, you could use your computer system—your Microsoft DOS, your Windows—to start connecting using primitive modems. But in the early days, I was so intrigued with the Commodore 64 that for one of my junior high school projects I decided to develop a program to calculate how many years a person might hypothetically live. Like I said, I was intrigued! My curiosity was unstoppable.

The way this program worked was based on assigning certain rates to different traits. People who smoked got a certain number of points. If a person is obese, that's a certain number of points. If a person is a diabetic, that's a certain number of points. And so on. Basically, I developed a simple program for life expectancy.

During the science fair, everyone was intrigued, and our table was crowded with participants asking questions. How does the system actually do this? How does it calculate? Does it make its own decisions? How does it decide? Of course, little did they know that everything was already pre-programmed. It wasn't anything sophisticated. For certain health traits, you have minus three years, plus two years. But it got so much attention. I was the brightest kid at the science fair!

For me, this was an "aha!" moment. This was the moment when I became really curious, wondering what this machine was capable of. What could this machine do in the future? Would it be able to take notes for us? Would it be able to do massive computational operations? Was it going to give us guidance in terms of where we travel? Was it going to communicate with other parts of the world? Could we send letters with it? What else would it be able to do?

Years later, we were able to start communicating using modem technologies. They didn't have any graphics and were still black, white, or green text on screens. But we were able to send some emails and correspond with people in a few other places or universities in the United States and the world.

This was the time that DARPA had just completed a project with an incredible pioneer, Dr. Vint Cerf (who I met later in 2005 in New York on the opening night of the famous PerSe restaurant), along with his colleague Bob Kahn, who created TCP/IP, which is the backbone of the way we communicate and layer things in a network.

Once they started creating this layering system of TCP/IP, some people across the United States became very intrigued. I was one of those people, and I purchased a then very expensive service from an Internet provider. I was using it to communicate, send some email, or get some information regarding travel. But everything was so primitive. We didn't have any visuals at that time.

Still, that was the third "aha!" moment for me. I became intrigued not only by how the systems are designed, but how we could communicate—when do you communicate, how do you get responses? How do our messages go through the telephone line?

When I entered university, my focus was computer science. I was interested not just in programming, but in understanding everything about the machine—how it was designed, how it was built, how machines are scaled, how they store information in the short term and the long term. I was intrigued by different programming languages. I was intrigued by big computing systems. At that time, a lot of big mainframes were very popular, and I got to understand how mainframe systems really work and what they bring to the table.

All of those "aha!" moments combined to bring me to where I am today. The first was when I was introduced to the Commodore 64, the second was when I created a life expectancy application for my school's science fair project, and the third was all about computer communication: being able to try different service providers and communicating through data. Before this, everything was about calling people, but now we were actually using data and computers to communicate without the need of voice.

Needing to Know the Why

Years later, I ended up at Comcast Cable Vision, which today is still one of the largest and most amazing cable companies in the world, let alone the United States. Comcast had acquired a number of small companies, and I got a job as a developer and IT junior manager. They put me in this room and basically said, "Okay, here's a project for you. Just deliver the results. Look at how many call logs people are doing with customer service, how many dropped calls, all of that stuff." And I said to myself, I want to understand the business. I want to understand the why: Why are we doing it?

But people would say, "Well, you're just a techie guy. Just sit there in the corner and do what we're asking you to do. You don't need to think. Just focus on your technology, on communications, and on your ability to leverage your computer science background to solve problems. We business people will tell you what to do and how to do it, and you just make it happen."

After my time at Comcast, I was hired by an Israeli startup that had received a significant amount of venture capital from an investor and was expanding. It was the first company to combine data and voice to be used in the business world, and you could actually send data messages and communicate on a mobile phone. I remember that this was a revolutionary product, where you could send communication to a company's truck drivers and they would respond to you, or you could text them or send some little apps.

It was very intriguing. But again, I was in a technical role, and everybody was telling me, Mark, do this and don't do this, don't question us, you don't really understand the business. At that point I got really angry.

I got so angry and I thought, I want to make a difference. I need to understand how the business world works. Who are we? Why are we doing this? Who is it benefiting? Is that the right approach? Why is it that the people who have MBAs are the ones who are going to tell us what to do and how to do it?

So I had gotten frustrated by that point and I thought, yes, I understand technology, I'm a computer scientist. But I've got to get an MBA and I've got to understand the business aspects of the issues, not only business prospects.

In those early years, I was already thinking that it's not enough just to understand the technical and business aspects; you also need to understand how people benefit. What is it for society? What do people get out of it? If you have this advanced data and voice technology, how do we make people's lives better? How do we make the truck driver's life better? How do they communicate better? Do we improve their safety? What do we do?

I was always thinking that there is a parallel universe that is not just made up of technology where you're told what to do, you don't have a brain, you're just doing tasks and pushing buttons. You need to understand the business so that it connects in your mind and you know why you're doing things.

I was always thinking that it all also has to have a societal element. Somebody has to be helped: people are suffering. Some consequence has to occur. All of those were amazing triggers for me related to why I really got more involved with science and technology.

Why Me, Why This Book?

This book is very, very important.

The biggest transformation in the world is occurring now on the digital front. That is where 60% to 65% of the global GDP is based: the digital supply chain, digital products, digital services, digital companies, digital governments. It's going to become a higher and higher percentage.

At some point, governments are going to digitize. I was fortunate and more than happy to contribute to the work of digital government at the United Nations. Digital government, also known as e-government, refers to the use of information and communication technologies (ICTs) to transform traditional government processes and service delivery models.

The UN has recognized the potential of digital government to accelerate progress toward achieving the Sustainable Development Goals (SDGs) by promoting efficient and effective governance, improving access to information and services, and fostering citizen participation and engagement.

This was a revolutionary transformation in governance. On the other hand, the power of digital has made the largest technology companies in the world as powerful as countries. I'm talking about Amazon, Alphabet, Meta, Apple, and Alibaba.

Data is the new oil. But data without meaning is not powerful. You need data that is qualified and quantified with reliable and unbiased intelligence and the information to know what to do with it and how to make solutions out of it.

The bottom line is that the world is shifting dramatically to a place where digital companies and digital enterprises have incredible amounts of power and will continue to gain even more. The reports indicate that about 52% to 54% of the workforce in the next several years is going to be digitally based, not based on physical/manual labor.

So with all of those factors, we now have to consider: Are we going to invest in massive digital transformations and massive digital transitions that are going on across the world only for the sake of profits, only for efficiency, only for optimization, and only for effectiveness?

I believe we need to change that paradigm. We now must create a different world: a world where people, citizens, societies, and human beings benefit from this massive technology spending and out of the massive progress that has been made. Humans must be the main consideration over profits, wealth, and efficiencies.

As the great writer Aldous Huxley so prophetically wrote, "The worst enemy of life, freedom, and the common decencies is total anarchy; their second worst enemy is total efficiency."

We must instead ask of the digitization of the world: How can it help us with our daily routines, with our daily problems both in life and at work, and with our health, our environment, and our societies? I looked around, and I didn't see anyone who truly converges the world of social innovation and impact with the world of digital and AI.

We have begun to have a major emphasis on responsible business practices and environments through the implementation of responsible AI. We have written a Bill of Rights for AI on what AI can and should not do and what is ethical or unethical.

We have regulations based on this Bill of Rights. There's a series of discussions and dialogue about ethical uses of AI, and where AI shouldn't be used—in health, military, or other activities, like surveillance, for example.

But something is still missing. The world needs someone who has deep technological and digital knowledge, as well as deep philosophical and global thinking, to look at where our world is going from a philosophical, futuristic perspective.

We need somebody who has spent time dealing with investments and looking at companies, policies, and regulations, as well as entrepreneurial aspects of the business world. We need someone to combine these aspects to understand how we address the issue of navigating and rerouting technology and digitalization toward the focus of positive and sustainable impact on the global society.

For all human beings. For all of us. For all people on this planet. People who are already at the last stage of life, and people who are beginning their journey. Who are just born. And people who are Gen Z and Millennials.

People across the world need a new way; we need a different framework. When we look at the corporate world, it is still stuck on increasing efficiency, effectiveness, optimization, profits, and quarterly returns.

I want to navigate this narrative, this book, toward how corporations, businesses, and the private sector can take advantage of massive digital transformation to drive revenue while simultaneously rerouting their energies and focus to create positive impacts on society.

These massive corporations have the power to work with governments to ensure that we have clean water and breathable air. We all know that we're facing the massive crisis of our time, climate change. We need to figure out how we can get to net zero in the best, most effective way possible. We have to figure out how we mitigate problems. We have to figure out how we adopt our current systems to better the planet. We have to figure out how we remove carbon from our environment. All of those solutions require digitalization and technology.

We can't have two or three separate worlds out there. We don't live in parallel universes. We live on one planet, and we need to make sure it can be home to sustainable human inhabitation. We hope to have a planet flourishing for the next generation, for our kids, for our grandkids, and for the future to come.

When I travel across the world, I see countries such as Switzerland and Japan that are focusing a lot of energy on having sustainable, energy-efficient transportation. I see countries focusing on efficiency and automation as well. And I see countries that are not focusing on any of that. They are only focusing on their own ability to survive. They want to create a life that benefits them, but no one else.

But what about others in the community? I've listed the issues that are very dear to me. Climate, health, infrastructure, education—the list goes on and on. A lot of them are listed at the United Nations and are part of the UN SDGs. But we don't have a way of connecting all of them.

The question is, how can we channel and route all of the many good things that are coming out of digital technology and the digitalization automation movement to better the human race as a whole? The data that is being generated will be able to help us produce products, services, frameworks, and capabilities that will be society-friendly. They are going to give us better predictions of weather events. They are going to help us with the prediction, prevention, and treatment of diseases, cancers, health scares, and pandemics. This data will help nurture more sustainable biodiversity. It will help us create a clean water supply. It will help us build better infrastructure so we can travel smarter and more energy-efficiently. All of these things are where the movement has to be: the moment of combining the entire digital world.

My Inspiration

When I travel, I meet spectacular people who motivate me and give me hope that the future will be amazing. I have met people like an entrepreneur from Norway who has been involved all his life in making Earth a little bit better, a little bit greener, and looking at ways to do this in places like India or other parts of the world.

I look at the work that is occurring when I travel to Japan. Many companies in Japan are committed to doing great things for society. Whole industries are being born in Japan that are focused on society and social innovation. The Japanese started Society 5.0, which I've written about extensively in prior years. When I travel to places like Switzerland and Norway and Japan, I get excited that there are people and leaders who are exploring different methods and different systems to create a better society, a better future.

What I mean by this is a society that works for all of us. A society that is inclusive. A society that gives benefits to every person and doesn't leave anyone behind. A society that is also in touch with nature and with natural elements, with our energy systems.

Recently I had a chance to visit the Kingdom of Saudi Arabia, and I was impressed with their strategy and vision for creating a digital society while having smart, sustainable cities that resulted in a better environment. They reinvest in the future so they'll have security and safety built in.

The Saudi models of smart sustainable cities—they call them giga projects—are truly inspirational.

We could make a great living, we could show resilience, we could show agility, we could show great key performance indicators in businesses that are aiming to help humans live a better life. Those companies themselves would be able to provide a better environment for employees who work in them.

We need one sustainable planet: one holistic approach where we don't just focus on making profits and efficiencies, but where we also take care of the things that really matter to the survival of the human race: from health to infrastructure, from transportation to logistics and to climate. We need to push the digital frameworks and digital methodologies and processes directly into that sphere of influence.

Then we will have a better future. A future for all of us. A future we can be proud to be the architects of.

Prologue

As I write this over the winter of 2022 to 2023, it's important to discuss some significant trends I'm seeing in the marketplace that make this book so crucial. We've witnessed a massive Russian invasion, the aftershocks of a global pandemic, economic challenges, climate challenges in the extreme, the evolution of major technology accelerations, and so on. You might think that we can't predict anything. However, something big is happening in the area of digital transformation that we must take note of.

It All Works Together

AI is not the same technology it was years ago. Now we have a combination of technologies called *transformative technologies* working closely together. These include AI, Internets of Things (IoTs), 5G technology, virtual and augmented reality, the cloud, blockchains, nonfungible tokens (NFTs), and the metaverse. The bottom line is that they don't work in isolation; they work as part of a stack. We cannot look at any technology in silos. Think of it like the movement in health to whole-person health, a concept that emphasizes the interconnectedness of an individual's physical, mental, emotional, and spiritual well-being. Everything works together to contribute to the soundness of the whole.

These solutions are now engraved deeply in the business world and governments worldwide, all supporting each other and creating efficiency that helps people every day. Businesses and large enterprises are leveraging all these technologies, not only in R&D and IT but also in operations.

There is no excuse for why AI and all of those digital technologies should not be used right now to create more value and more demand.

These technologies will provide better customer service, more efficiency, better products, quality services, and more efficient supply chains. They are going to be more aligned with customer experiences and customer intimacy. They will streamline financial processes. They will streamline manufacturing and logistics. The barriers to access will be less and less. All of those technologies are now not only available as a product or stand-alone but also as a service model. You can get them on the cloud, on demand, via some technology, or through some app.

Resilience Through Adaptation

Companies and enterprises around the world have to figure out how to take resilience to the next level. How do you get resilience when it comes to market volatility? What kind of protective mechanisms can you put on supply chains and value chains against shortages and rising costs? How do you mitigate risks? How do you become more self-reliant?

Beyond 2023, environmental, social, and governance (ESG) nonfinancial factors are going to move to the center from the political and scientific extremes. Businesses will have to focus strategy on environmental and social needs, not simply revenue and profit and loss.

The Japanese are way ahead of their time. During my trip to Japan in 2019 to participate in B20/G20, I remember seeing firsthand and learning about Society 5.0 (proposed by the Japanese government in 2016, it is a concept for the future of society, which aims to combine advances in technology with the values of human-centered society). From transparency to reporting to accountability, every business, large or local, needs to do this to remain competitive and thrive going forward in the twenty-first century. All levels of businesses need to understand that society matters, and people are part of society. We need certain levels of healthcare, we need to have a good climate, and we require a healthy environment.

In the Pages to Come

Whether it be the 30,000-foot view of sustainability, customer experiences, talent acquisition, and digital labor, or the transformation and evolution of healthcare, artificial intelligence and the ethical implementation and use thereof will be the key driver to a brighter, cleaner, and more holistic future for every business, consumer, man, woman, and child on planet Earth.

In the pages to come, I will share actionable ways for you to work toward a sustainable planet using AI in your personal and professional life. Please take your time in reading and making notes on this book. The stories, details, studies, and direction that follow could be the difference between a healthy life, business, and environment, or you being passed by and swallowed up by your competitors.

PART

I

AI's Impact on Modern Work and Life

Artificial intelligence (AI) plays a distinct and significant role in our society and holds immense potential for our future. Despite concerns that AI may lead to job displacement, its global impact is undeniable. The digital transformation driven by AI is enabling businesses and industries to become more efficient and productive, ultimately creating more capacity to accomplish more work in less time. Undoubtedly, AI and digital technology are driving progress toward a better and more efficient world. However, detractors continue to voice their concerns, particularly in areas such as language models.

As an illustration, the creative industry in Delhi is among those expressing concern about the impact of AI on employment opportunities, while fast food chains and call centers face similar challenges posed by chatbots and automation. The advent of cognitive agents has resulted in the displacement of roles previously performed by human operators, who were tasked with addressing customer inquiries and resolving billing issues.

The consequences of such shifts are being closely scrutinized, with the emergence of new AI models such as OpenAI's Chat GPT garnering attention due to their ability to engage in human-like conversations and provide direct and informative responses. While some may perceive these developments as exacerbating unemployment, the reality is that employment figures may remain low due to competition in other areas and increasing automation. Furthermore, it is possible that individuals may not be interested in pursuing roles within call centers or fast food establishments, and may instead seek alternative career paths. Ultimately, the impact of AI on employment remains a complex issue with varied implications across different sectors.

From a broader perspective, digital transformation enables individuals to utilize their cognitive abilities to a greater extent. In our economy, we have jobs that are considered less significant and not sustainable over the long term. These roles can be effectively performed by robots or automated agents, which raises the question of why humans must undertake these tasks. In times of crisis, such as during the recent pandemic, some jobs are challenging to perform, requiring the use of robots in situations such as rescue operations in remote or inaccessible locations. In the hospitality industry, there may be insufficient human resources to fulfill certain roles. In such cases, automation can help fill the gap. It is important to acknowledge that certain jobs may not be available due to a lack of skilled workers, making automation a feasible solution for some industries.

In many countries, including the United States, there are gaps that we cannot fill with human workers alone, and we must be careful in addressing these gaps. The job of a truck driver, for example, is no longer just about driving a truck. We now require that truck drivers be able to operate complex systems that we can communicate with effectively, similar to the way traffic controllers manage airplane traffic. Perhaps the future of truck driving will involve drivers sitting in virtual simulations while the truck drives itself, so that they can avoid accidents and enjoy a more pleasant work experience.

Likewise, we can leverage AI to improve efficiency in the fast food and hotel industries. Instead of relying on young people to perform menial tasks, we can use AI to clean hotel rooms and let machines handle customer service calls. Of course, we need to ensure that AI does not discriminate based on age, gender, or race, and we must work to eliminate biases and ensure fairness.

AI has great potential to help us solve societal problems, such as building better transportation infrastructure, fighting diseases, and improving our food supply chain. While we do not want machines to replace humans entirely, we need to find a proper balance of augmentation so that humans and AI can work together as a team to contribute to society. It is also important to note that new jobs will be created, such as repairing IoT devices and dealing with large amounts of data.

To compete with China, we need to use AI and automation to our advantage. We must leverage these technologies to complement human efforts in military technology, energy, and infrastructure. In the future, simulations will play an increasingly important role in solving global problems, such as climate change. We can use digital twins to simulate major surgeries and building construction to improve accuracy and efficiency. Visualization and communication tools, such as infographics and digital twins, will help us convey complex information in the most effective and accurate manner.

1 | Current Challenges and Issues with AI

This chapter covers how Big Tech is driving artificial intelligence to the next stage of evolution.

What Is Artificial Intelligence?

Let's level-set to start. *Artificial intelligence* is a term that is thrown around often and that is seemingly interchangeable with similar ones like *machine learning* or *deep learning*. To demystify the composition of AI and its technology, let's begin by describing the differences between those three terms.

To start, there are two types of AI: *artificial general intelligence* (AGI) and *artificial narrow intelligence* (ANI). Artificial general intelligence is what you read about in science-fiction novels and what you see in science-fiction movies; it is a machine's ability to think and develop the same cognitive abilities that a human being has. When you hear people talk about AI today, however, they are usually referring to the latter of the two, artificial narrow intelligence. As for the rest of the book, when we reference AI, we will be speaking specifically about ANI, which in today's world is ubiquitous. Artificial narrow intelligence is a specific type of artificial intelligence that is goal-oriented and that tackles a particular set of tasks. *Machine learning* is a type of AI that can automatically adapt with minimal human interference, while *deep learning* is a subset of machine learning that is based on artificial neural networks that mimic the learning process of the human mind.

How did we get to where we are today, with respect to the evolution of AI?

I would argue that most inventions begin in the depths of the human imagination and then make a debut appearance in society through science fiction. And most thoughts begin with questions: What if we could get there faster? What if there was a better way to search for things? What if things could act like humans? The common thread that holds these questions together is efficiency.

During the Second Industrial Revolution (aka the Technological Revolution), at what I would say is the peak of human ingenuity, the development of the railroad system did an amazing thing. It opened the way for expansion in the West, provided new economic opportunities, stimulated the development of towns and communities, and tied the country together: *It was making life efficient.* During this time, machines took on a central role in making the lives of people easier whether through alleviating manual labor, simplifying transportation, or providing entertainment. But that was only the beginning.

The question "Can machines think?" began rattling the minds of people during the Golden Age of Science Fiction, which started in 1938. Evidence for this can first be seen in the silent film *Metropolis*, a 1927 German expressionist film that starred a female humanoid robot. Man's curiosity toward robots and an early concept of artificial intelligence was awakened and culturally embedded, sparking a quest for knowledge and the beginning stages of AI.

In 1951 the earliest successful AI program was written by Christopher Strachey, and by the summer of 1952, this program could play a complete game of checkers. Three years later, in 1955, Arthur Samuel figured out a way to add features that would enable Strachey's program to learn from experience. In 1970, Marvin Minsky and Seymour Papert of the MIT AI lab proposed that AI research should focus on developing programs that are capable of intelligent behavior in artificial environments known as *microworlds*.

Today, AI is ubiquitous, and it can outperform human experts when it comes to narrow fields. AI is used in detecting medical diagnoses, genetic engineering, early cancer detection, and even protein folding, and that is just naming a few fields in biomedicine. AI is used for chemical analysis, car design and manufacturing, bridge design, airline scheduling, customer service, ad targeting, and so much more.

Deep learning has been one of the most significant breakthroughs in AI since the mid 2010s because it has radically reduced the amount of manual labor and effort that is involved in building artificial intelligence systems. The rapid expansion and use of deep learning has been made possible through the growing access to big data and cloud architectures that allow massive amounts of data to be used to train complex AI models.[1]

What Is Big Tech?

This section covers the importance of Big Tech and its control and reach within our society, community, startups, and enterprises.

Big Tech refers to the most dominant and influential companies that exist in the technology industry (these companies exist mostly within the United States). These Big Tech corporations are now entering the public domain, but they have a unique advantage that no other corporations share: access to the data of billions of users.

This access allows them to design business models that are reliant on a private source of information that can be used to sell data, design a product based on the user data, or target particular groups of people and potential buyers based on the data they've collected. Since Big Tech corporations have access to large data sets and a vast number of resources, they have become systems that not only provide services, but entire infrastructures.[2,3]

"Indeed, such corporations exercise control on essential services on which many different actors and the whole economic ecosystem depend."[4,5] Moreover, scholars have maintained that in this way, Big Tech corporations may have not only substantial economic and market power but a political "platform power" that stems directly from their consumers and users, who intimately appreciate and rely on those corporations and tend to provide opposition to governmental regulations that treat such corporations' convenience and innovation.[6]

My Hands-on Experience in Big Tech

I began my professional journey as a programmer, which laid the foundation for my training in computer science and engineering. Over the course of my career, I have gained valuable experience working at Comcast, IBM, and US Web, to name a few. In the early 1990s, technology was viewed primarily as a tool, and there was a need to delve into every detail, often requiring specialized knowledge and expertise.

At that time, it was difficult to connect the dots, as everything was isolated and parochial, and the Internet was still in its nascent stage. The development of applications was largely siloed, and personalization and preferences were not yet integrated. Building technology was a complex and expensive process, with limited impact on society beyond the realm of engineering.

Fast forward to today, and the landscape has transformed dramatically. Technology has become more accessible, affordable, and ubiquitous. As a result, computer power has become more affordable and easier to understand. In the past, engineers were the primary drivers of technological solutions, which limited accessibility and communication to a broader audience. Now, technology is simpler and more integrated, which benefits members of society across age groups and industries.

Big Tech and data are so pervasive that they control our lives and our destiny. To illustrate this, over two-thirds of Americans obtain their news from social media platforms such as Facebook and the more alarming TikTok, which is controlled by China and impacts young minds. Nine out of 10 people follow someone or share something from their network on social media.

Companies like Alphabet (Google) and Meta (Facebook) are now some of the biggest on the Fortune 500 list, and YouTube, which is owned by Google, is the most popular video site globally.

This widespread adoption has made tracking our daily movements much more effortless, as seen through the use of Google Maps on our phones. Even if we go to the hospital, we can be monitored through Apple Watches, which report our oxygen, heart rate, pulse, and temperature data to the cloud. This plethora of data is now in the hands of Big Tech, which can utilize it as they please, giving them enormous power over us. In addition, Big Tech is now intertwined with every aspect of our lives, even controlling the way we live our lives.

The power wielded by these companies is unprecedented, and it remains unclear whether we should allow them to monopolize and maximize their profits or regulate them through ethical guidelines. Despite the current challenges faced by the technology sector, Big Tech remains a powerful entity in 2023, and its business models continue to consume organizations and daily living.

All aspects of our lives are being meticulously monitored and documented. This prompts us to question whether this is the direction we want to be headed in. The renowned Harvard professor Shoshana Zuboff, in her 2002 book *The Support Economy: Wealth, Work, and Careers in the Knowledge Economy*, predicted a model whereby we are integrated into a social community, exchanging information and ideas. This new society will be immensely powerful, surpassing traditional employment and family structures. Is that where we are now?

This seamless integration of our lives is epitomized by the tech giants Amazon, Google (Alphabet), Facebook (Meta), Microsoft, and Apple, who are intricately woven into the fabric of our daily routines.

Within the hospital system, there are beds equipped with tracking mechanisms for patient safety, such as fall prevention. Additionally, Apple Watches have capabilities to track vital signs including oxygen levels, heart rate, and body temperature, which are all stored in the cloud. With an abundance of data being collected, the largest tech companies have the ability to utilize this information as they see fit. Consequently, we are at the mercy of these companies, and even if we have done no wrong, they may sever ties with us based on a statement we make.

It is important to note that personal information and accounts are under their control, and as technology advances, AI agents may be the ones responsible for sensing and controlling our daily activities, managing our authentication process, and dictating our connectivity.

The omnipotence of Big Tech is truly remarkable, for better or for worse. While social media platforms provide exceptional services, and Microsoft offers a wide array of exceptional products, the costs to our society are significant. Are we prepared to bear the burden of such commitments and obligations to Big Tech? These organizations possess more power than any Wall Street companies ever have.

How We Coexist with Big Tech

As we navigate these challenging times, we must consider how we wish to coexist with Big Tech. Should we regulate their actions and maximize their profits, or allow for innovation and new startups to thrive? It is essential to consider how AI ethics play into this discussion.

Moreover, as we become increasingly reliant on connected devices, such as the generative AI Chat GPT or self-driving cars, we must contemplate the effects of Big Tech's involvement. Microsoft's partnership and investment in OpenAI, for instance, could mean that they distribute and control generative AI Chat GPT, leading to unforeseen consequences.

The present and future impact of Big Tech on society is a subject of great importance, with significant ethical implications. The European Union and UNESCO are engaged in discussions on AI ethics, raising questions about the optimal balance between profit maximization and the avoidance of monopolies that stifle innovation. The partnership and investment of Microsoft in OpenAI and their distribution and control of generative AI Chat GPT is one example of the significant influence Big Tech wields over the use of AI technologies.

However, the question arises: How do we trust this technology, particularly in terms of privacy? Issues related to AI bias, fairness, fraud, and misrepresentation are prevalent. Moreover, Big Tech companies control a broad swath of our lives, including what we think, the healthcare we receive, the diagnostics we undergo, our communications, our travel, our food intake, and even the restaurants we frequent.

This immense power is comparable to that of authoritarian regimes in China and Russia. The tendencies toward control and domination are embedded in the new world of Big Tech, which seeks to regulate every aspect of society and culture. Consequently, we must exercise caution because our lives are so heavily intertwined with these technologies. Even an hour of disconnection can lead to a feeling of deprivation because we have become so reliant on them.

This raises important questions for society, particularly younger generations who are growing up in this increasingly digital world. Do we truly want content on demand and everything at lightning-fast speeds, even if it comes at the expense of our privacy and time? We must be mindful of the implications of these developments and work toward creating a balance that prioritizes ethical considerations and the common good.

The Dominance of Big Data

The issue of data exploitation and the power held by large technology companies is a significant concern. It is imperative to strike a balance between the desire for efficiency and speed, and the need to prevent unelected corporations from having excessive control over every aspect of our lives.

The dominance of these companies, which are larger than life, necessitates careful consideration. Governments, especially in the United States, are summoning them to Congress, and discussions about regulations are taking place, especially in the European Union.

The issue at hand is the limitation of power held by the largest technology companies, who exert significant pressure on society by providing content and information, while simultaneously gaining access to vast amounts of data. The challenge lies in finding ways to utilize this knowledge and network to amplify human voices, especially given the advancements in generative AI and monitoring technology that could act as "whisper agents," monitoring our emotions and brain activity.

This has significant implications for our economy, as the largest tech companies hold substantial economic leverage and control over many aspects of our lives. It's important to consider the influence these companies have on democracy, voting, innovation, politics, and religious beliefs. As citizens, consumers, employees, and employers, it's critical that we navigate this landscape thoughtfully and with care, given the immense power wielded by these digital superpowers.

We must examine all facets of this issue, including privacy concerns, the potential impact on jobs, and the displacement of workers. We must balance innovation, efficiency, and effectiveness with governance, regulations, democracy, and politics.

It is crucial to ensure that power does not swing in a direction where individuals suddenly find themselves powerless due to the dominance of these tech giants. We must establish a trust system and develop a new society that takes into account the technological advantage these companies possess. This requires collective and careful consideration.

Gen Z's Evolving Digital Transformation

Millennials are a main driver of digital transformation in the twenty-first-century workplace. More than 40% of millennials say they won't work for organizations that don't offer workplace and work-from-home flexibility.[7] The younger generations in the workforce and currently joining the workforce only know a world where they can work from anywhere. Many of them put flexibility above wages and benefits when prioritizing what organization they will work for.

Enterprises globally have no path forward except to adapt. Top talent knows they will get the flexibility somewhere and will not settle. Any work that can securely be performed remotely must be offered as such. A failure by a company to evolve with top talent will leave them behind their competitors who have embraced the future and changed with the times. Just do a quick Google search for companies that failed to adapt to changing technologies. What happened to them? You'll see names like MySpace, Blockbuster, Commodore, Kodak, Polaroid, and the list goes on. Hesitation leads to devastation.

AI Will Augment Humanity, Not Replace It

As written about in the *Harvard Business Review*, a study of 1,500 companies revealed that businesses achieve the most significant performance improvements when humans and machines work together.[8] People and AI actively complement the strengths of the other. Humans lead the way in leadership, teamwork, creativity, and social skills, while AI brings speed, scalability, and quantitative capabilities needed to maximize output and performance.

On the most basic levels, humans are needed to maintain machines, repair, and improve them. Humans are also the ones who tell machines where to start and what to do. Humans must also code these machines to only perform tasks that are good in nature and do not harm people. We are also needed to explain and interpret the work of machines to the masses.

We have to acknowledge the ways in which machines help humans augment and enhance our abilities, whether it is cognitive—such as weeding out calls and requests to route them to the correct person, or answering their questions completely, or suggesting a different path for you—or, giving you needed answers to questions you didn't even think to ask. This use of AI makes our lives a little better and more efficient everyday. Yes, I know some of you reading this are saying, "Mark, I just want to talk to a person!" So do I, but I like a cognitive agent making sure I reach the correct person, and not just someone who is going to transfer me to someone else who is going to transfer me!

Digital Transformation and Personalization

People, not machines, drive innovation. Technology isn't created or advanced just for the fun of it. The genesis of all innovation has been the needs of people. One of the greatest demands of our time is personalization of products, services, and experiences. This happens every day without us even noticing.

Right now, if you take out your phone (of course, please wait until after this chapter) and open any app, you will see content and advertisements that are only for things and topics you are interested in, or are already a consumer of. This isn't an accident. This is from years of users of tech, like me and you, demanding and moving toward apps, companies, services, and experiences that are more tailored to what we like.

Gone are the days when you had to go look for something you wanted. One Google or Facebook search of "Men's coats near me" and immediately I start seeing ads, articles, and videos about men's coats. This makes my life more efficient, in a small way, yes, but more efficient nonetheless.

But the marketers behind these personalized advertising campaigns must be the ones who understand what we actually want. "Top marketers are developing systems that can pool and analyze structured and unstructured data, algorithms that can identify behavioral patterns and customer propensity, and analysis capabilities to feed that information into easy-to-use dashboards."[9]

Again, this is all driven by us.

- 91% of consumers say they are more likely to shop with brands that provide offers and recommendations that are relevant to them.
- 83% of consumers are willing to share their data to create a more personalized experience.
- Consumers are 2.1 times more likely to view personalized offers.
- 88% of US marketers have seen measurable improvements due to personalization, with more than half reporting a lift greater than 10%.
- Marketers report a 760% increase in email revenue from personalized and segmented campaigns.[10]

Recent AI Success Stories

What enhancements have the behavior of humans driven in AI in the recent past? There are too many to name in this chapter alone, but here are some that you may overlook in your everyday life that makes things easier, safer, and more cost effective:

- Virtual assistants reduce unnecessary hospital visits and save nurses 20% of their time. At the same time, workflow assistants free 17% of doctors' schedules.[11]

- AI is being used to predict when to book your vacation to get the lowest price for flights, hotels, car, and vacation home rentals.[12]
- Have you purchased anything on Amazon in the past five years? If so, their algorithm has helped you do so.
- Voice assistants, anyone? Before leaving your house you can simply yell out, "Alexa" or "Hey Google, what is the forecast today? How is the traffic on my commute?" You don't have to wait for the news to come back from a commercial break and hope they go straight to weather and traffic. You have that info exactly when you want it.

These are some small examples to show how human behaviors drive innovation. I need to know the weather as I leave the house, not when the news decides to tell me the weather. I want to get the best price on my family vacation to Miami. I want the more relevant products at the best price available shown to me when I am shopping on Amazon. These behaviors have driven the innovations we all use every day.

Now that you see how what you want and need can literally change the world, in Chapter 2 let's get into how the needs of the human race and planet Earth will continue to drive innovation and the advancement of AI.

2 | AI for Social Good

This chapter covers the implications of AI on the current crises of the planet.

Right now, AI is being leveraged across the world as a force for positive societal change, life-saving medical enhancements, reusable and sustainable energy, and securing the food supply chain. I show you in this chapter the ways in which AI is a force for good, a force for positive change, and a force that can save humanity and our planet.

Our global issues are complex, and AI provides us with a valuable tool to augment human efforts to come up with solutions to vexing problems. These challenges are new and old and they have the potential to touch every single one of our lives. In the pages to come, you will read about at least one, likely multiple, challenges you face in your life and how AI can be used to help us all conquer them.

Improving Municipal Efficiency

We take for granted the massive work and incredibly complex and inter-twined systems it takes for a city to function at all, let alone in the most efficient and citizen-friendly ways possible. Not only do residents and visitors need to get from one place to the next for work, dinner, a night out with friends, or a first date (or second, if you're lucky), people also need the city to work *for them* and their lives, because lives often depend on the ways a city actually functions. For example, a well-functioning city provides its residents with access to essential resources and services, such as healthcare, education, transportation, and affordable housing. This can help to ensure that everyone has the basic necessities they need to lead healthy and productive lives.

AI traffic networks have been proven to work to move people and public services in a more efficient and lifesaving way through a metropolitan area. For example, real-time traffic camera data and IoT are being leveraged to maximize vehicle throughput in cities.[1] Municipalities have the ability as well to harness the power of AI to decide when and where preventive maintenance of public transportation (trains, buses, subways, etc.) and infrastructure (bridges, roads, tunnels, etc.) should occur to prevent future disruptions and potential disasters.

Improving Energy Efficiency

We all see the news every summer here in the United States of rolling blackouts, or cities and regions losing power completely. This isn't just a modern inconvenience; this is something that kills hundreds, if not thousands, of people every year.

One example of rolling blackouts leading to deaths occurred in Texas during a severe winter storm in February 2021. As the storm swept across the state, record-low temperatures caused a surge in power demand, which overwhelmed the state's electrical grid. As a result, utility companies began implementing rolling blackouts, which left millions of Texans without power for hours at a time.

The prolonged blackouts had severe consequences for public health and safety, with many residents struggling to stay warm in the freezing temperatures. Some residents resorted to using unsafe heating methods, such as propane heaters and charcoal grills, which led to several cases of carbon monoxide poisoning. Others were left without access to clean water and sanitation, as water treatment plants and pumping stations were also affected by the power outages.

In total, over 100 deaths were attributed to the winter storm, with many of these deaths occurring as a result of the rolling blackouts. The incident highlighted the importance of resilient and reliable energy systems, as well as the need for better emergency planning and response measures to protect public health and safety during extreme weather events.

Artificial intelligence can be used in smart cities to analyze the energy-use habits and trends of businesses and residents. Analyzing this data informs decisions as to when and where renewable energy needs to be used. City planners gain insights as to where energy is being wasted and how to save it.[2] The next step is to install this tech in every city possible and scale it nationwide. We know the technology works. We know it will save money and, more importantly, lives. To not continue down this path is negligence on the part of our leaders and governments.

At Google, Ana Radovanovic, Technical Lead for Carbon-Intelligent Computing, is leading a project that studies electricity maps. These maps predict how the average hourly carbon intensity of the local electrical grid will change over the course of a day. Then this data is used to inform how to align compute tasks with times of low-carbon electricity supply.[3] Initial results show that carbon-aware load shifting works.

Detecting Cancer Early On

The imaging capabilities of AI are currently being leveraged in early-stage detection of cancerous cells and other diseases. A Mount Sinai team used deep learning–based AI algorithms to predict the development of diseases with 94% accuracy, including cancers of the liver, rectum, and prostate.[4]

The development of convolutional neural networks has massive life-saving potential. One convolutional neural network was trained on 130,000 skin images and was able to classify malignant lesions with higher sensitivity and specificity than doctors.

In addition, tumors in the head and neck cancer lymph nodes are difficult to diagnose radiographically. The convolutional neural network–based model showed greater than 85% accuracy in identifying this feature on CT scans.[5] Not only can this use of AI match the diagnostic powers of clinicians, and sometimes better than them, it also does it much faster. And when it comes to cancer and disease detection, time is so very valuable.

Enabling Smarter Living

Our lives can be very hectic. Personally, I travel constantly, nationally and internationally, and my amazing wife is the rock of our family at home, taking care of our daughter, taking care of our home, and monitoring our extended family. We, like so many people, need technology in our lives to help us every day, not just with the daily tasks of life, but with being safe and secure.

Smart living is a way many people approach their homes. Think of all of the AI-driven devices in our homes today:

- *Smart thermostats*: Keep our homes regulated and efficient.
- *Smart security system*: Keep our home secure and us up-to-date in real time as to any problems or danger while we are away.
- *Panic buttons for elderly or sick family members*: The ability to communicate in real time possible falls, injuries, and changes in health are literal life-savers.

Safety and security are fundamental drivers of smart living. These innovations, like all, are brought about by the needs and wants of people like you and me. Nowadays most of this tech is very affordable and becomes more so every year.

Fighting Climate Change

Machine learning algorithms power approximately 30 climate models used by the Intergovernmental Panel on Climate Change.[6] My colleagues at the Boston Consulting Group (BCG) and I agree that AI is essential in the fight to solve the climate crises. BCG has developed a common framework to combat climate change and is working on multiple fronts, leveraging AI to bring about positive change in the arena of climate change (see Figure 2.1).

In BCG's experience, for example, AI can be used to help reduce greenhouse gas emissions equal to 5–10% of an organization's carbon footprint, or a total of 2.6 to 5.3 gigatons of CO_2e if scaled globally.[7] AI can also be a tool for helping businesses, governments, nongovermental organizations, and investors take a more informed and data-driven approach in combating climate change at any level.

Supporting Wildlife Conservation

AI has been used in wildlife conservation in several ways. For example, the University of Hawaii's Kauai Endangered Seabird Recovery Project used AI to analyze 600 hours of audio to detect the number of collisions between birds and power lines.[8]

Also, AI has been used in the form of drones to help spot poachers and to track species and migration patterns. Drones are also being taught

Framework for Using AI to Combat Climate Change

	Mitigation			Adaptation and resilience		Fundamentals
TOPICS	Measurement	Reductions	Removal	Hazard forecasting	Vulnerability and exposure management	
SUBTOPICS AND EXAMPLES	Macro-level measurement e.g., estimating remote carbon natural stock Micro-level measurement e.g., calculating the carbon footprint of individual products	Reducing GHG emissions intensity e.g., supply forecasting for solar energy Improving energy efficiency e.g., encouraging behavioral change Reducing greenhouse effects e.g., accelerating aerosol and chemistry research	Environmental removal e.g., monitoring encroachment on forests and other natural reserves Technological removal e.g., assessing carbon-capture storage sites	Projecting regionalized long-term trends e.g., regionalized modeling of sea-level rise or extreme events such as wildfires and floods Building early warning systems e.g., near-term prediction of extreme events such as cyclones	Managing crises e.g., monitoring epidemics Strengthening infrastructure e.g., intelligent irrigation Protecting populations e.g., predicting large-scale migration patterns Preserving biodiversity e.g., identifying and counting species	Climate research and modeling e.g., modeling of economic and social transition Climate finance e.g., forecasting carbon prices Education, nudging, and behavioral change e.g., recommendations for climate-friendly consumption
USES FOR AI	Gather, complete, and process data · Satellite and IoT data · Filling gaps in temporally and spatially sparse data	Strengthen planning and decision making · Policy and climate-risk analytics · Modeling higher-order effects · Bionic management	Optimize processes · Supply chain optimization · Simulation environments	Support collaborative ecosystems · Vertical data sharing · Enhanced communication tools		Encourage climate-positive behaviors · Climate-weighted suggestions · Climate-friendly optimization functions

Note: GHG = greenhouse gas; IoT = Internet of Things.

Figure 2.1 Framework for using AI to combat climate change

Source: BCG project experience; Climate Change AI, "Tackling Climate Change with Machine Learning"; Global Partnership on AI, "Climate Change and AI: Recommendations for Government Action".

Expert Analysis: Work at BCG Is Responsibility and Contribution to the Betterment of Society

By Sylvain Duranton, Global Leader of BCG X, and Senior Partner and Managing Director of Boston Consulting Group

Why is it important for both you and your organization to ensure that the work not only generates revenue but also contributes to the betterment of society?

We feel a need and a responsibility to go beyond financial returns and consider the impact of our actions on society. For our organization, working with companies has always been about more than just numbers. We have been working with them for years to define their purpose, improve their social impact, and manage stakeholders.

However, technology has forced us to make more explicit and stronger decisions when it comes to trade-offs between financial gain and other considerations. Centralized decision-making through AI and technology means that we must decide on objective functions like cost, CO_2 emissions, worker and customer satisfaction, and team NPS. This is where our duty as BCG comes in—we need to ensure that it's not just about money, but also doing good for the world, our customers, and our teams.

We also have partnerships with organizations like the Green Software Foundation and Mila to push the tech sector toward responsible AI and responsible technologies. We believe that the influence we have on technology comes with a responsibility to behave in a way that is geared toward the greater good. Simply saying that "tech will save the world" is no longer enough, and we need to work toward improving ethical standards across the tech industry.

What do you think the future of climate tech looks like from your perspective?

There are several important aspects to consider. First, measurement is crucial. If companies want to tackle the climate crisis, they need to accurately measure their impact on the environment. While many companies are committed to reducing their emissions, most still struggle to measure them. A survey conducted two years ago found that the average company self-reported a 30–40% uncertainty in their own emissions measurements. To address this, we need to leverage AI and blockchain technologies to simulate and measure emissions from operations and supply chains.

The second aspect is decarbonization, which involves reducing carbon emissions from operations. This can be achieved through various means, including changing agricultural practices to store more carbon in the soil, using carbon capture technologies, and optimizing operations to reduce carbon emissions. For example, we have a procurement optimization solution that includes the price of CO_2 and optimizes both the cost of goods and their carbon emissions.

The third aspect is adaptation, which is just as important as decarbonization. As we see the impacts of climate change worsen, we need to plan for and mitigate its effects. This involves using AI and optimization to forecast climate risks and plan for them accordingly. For example, cities can use digital twins to optimize their infrastructure and prepare for upcoming climate challenges, such as flooding. This requires quantifying the costs of infrastructure and social impacts, such as the displacement of people, and optimizing decision-making across different departments and time horizons.

The future of climate tech requires advanced technology and innovative solutions to accurately measure emissions, reduce carbon emissions, and adapt to climate risks.

to locate waste materials floating in or on the water and then to notify a marine animal conservation agency for cleanup.

Combating the Food Crisis

The fact that kids go to bed hungry every night, people are literally starving across the globe, and people die every day from not having food may be the greatest tragedy of our time. From food deserts to climate struggle to

Expert Input and Analysis: Hitachi Must Use Its Influence and Access to AI to Positively Impact Climate Change

By Laurent Guengant, Vice President—Global Environmental Business Division—Head of EMEA Corporate Venture—at Hitachi

Global companies like Hitachi are instrumental in enabling and accelerating the green transition (mitigation), as well as addressing the consequences of climate change (adaptation).

Hitachi, and other global companies, have to face and address the strategic and economic challenges generated by an accelerated environmental transition. These include managing legacy assets and cost structures, optimizing transformation costs, and achieving price and "value" competitiveness for new and greener products. Hitachi believes in a bright Green future and has been focusing its investments in technologies that drive this transition toward new market opportunities. As a global multinational corporation, it is also well positioned to create the economies of scales needed for this transition. Through a large customer base, reach, and global mind share, it has a greater potential for effectively supporting customers in their migration to the new zero-carbon-based technologies, solutions, and business models. Last, but not least, with very large employee bases, Hitachi and other global corporations are instrumental in designing and driving larger-scale industry and value chain-wide reskilling and upskilling programs for workers.

From an adaptation standpoint, global infrastructure solutions providers such as Hitachi have been investing significantly in new AI models to address the risks caused by climate change. Some of the areas of focus include AI models for the design of more resilient infrastructures, the improved security of energy supply, but also for the modeling and prediction of natural disaster scenarios, such as sea-level-rise modeling, early warning systems, or risk and insurance models.

It is important also to note that global companies' influence goes beyond their employees and reaches their employees' families and communities. Through this extended market and community access, they are well positioned, often in partnerships with local authorities, to implement educational programs aimed at changing behaviors, preparing populations, and providing tools to better address the impacts of climate change.

Positive impact on inequality, accessibility to basic needs, and combating food crises

Most large global corporations also have strong diversity and inclusion programs. As global corporations implement mitigation of adaptation-focused programs, key criteria for success of these programs include accessibility, affordability, efficient utilization of natural resources, and supporting public and nonprofit organizations dedicated to improving the well-being of citizens.

Hitachi's work in AI positively impacting the field of energy sustainability

In recent years, Hitachi has built new businesses in the electro-mobility sector, leveraging AI to implement more efficient use of lithium-ion batteries (battery analytics), and optimizing the second-life reusability of these batteries. For electric and hybrid commercial fleets, the use of AI models was extended to the optimization of routes and charging schedules, as well as the modeling of driver behaviors in order to optimize bus and delivery trucks' battery usage. Other new applications of AI for Hitachi include the development of more flexible and resilient energy grids and the automation of distributed multi-energy resources.

political strife and war, the factors fueling the global food crises are many and varied. AI is poised to help in many ways and save countless lives.

For example, the Nutrition Early Warning System uses machine learning and big data to identify regions that are at increased risk of food shortages due to crop failure, rising food prices, and drought.[9] AI is being leveraged in the area of farm management and predictive analytics. Using data from crop, soil, and weather monitoring, AI can support decision-making to optimize the use of resources (water, fertilizers, etc.).[10]

This is the direction we need to continue to head in. If on a global scale we can predict when disaster is likely to hit and where and to whom, we can manage production and distribution of food to lessen the impact on people.

With the technology currently available on this planet, it is an utter failure of humanity that global hunger continues to exist.

Reducing Inequity

Most of us have deep-coded biases that we don't even know are there. AI can help save people like you and me from mistakes we'd never dream of making, and save us all from malicious actors out there being intentionally biased. Take, for example, smart text editor Textio. Textio is used to rewrite job descriptions to make them more inclusive. This leads to a more diverse candidate pool, which leads to a more diverse workforce, which leads to more diverse and inclusive viewpoints at an organization. In turn, this will lead to organizations reducing or eliminating all hidden unintentional biases.

From preventing biases, we need to remove existing biases. The recent development of open source toolkits such as the University of Chicago's project Aequitas and IBM's AI Fairness 360 is a wonderful step forward. They both track and correct existing biases. They use a comprehensive set of metrics for datasets and models to test for biases, explanations for these metrics, and algorithms to mitigate bias in datasets and models.[11] These sorts of systems are crucial in rooting out and correcting biases, whether they be intentional or not.

Let's also look at how and from whom we get our news. We need to ensure that the voices and faces we see are a fair representation of the community they are serving. The best way to reach this result is by first assessing where a change is needed. Swiss multimedia publishing business Ringier is working on this challenge by leveraging AI to monitor the gender bias of its output via a tool the company developed, EqualVoice. It analyzes the number of men and women that appear in their articles, features, and clips.

Improving Education

AI is being used in education in several ways. The first is to make the work of educating more efficient. AI has been implemented in the creation of course materials, automating mundane tasks to take them off the educators, and providing additional opportunities for virtual learning.

AI is also being used to help students and create individual learning paths. Take, for example, the organization SDG4. Sustainable Development Goal 4 is about quality education and is among the 17 Sustainable Development Goals (SDGs) established by the United Nations in September 2015. The full title of SDG 4 is "Ensure inclusive and equitable quality education and promote lifelong learning opportunities for AI." We see AI being used to help determine the comfort level of children in learning different subjects, and to identify struggling pupils without having to wait for scores and grades.

Improving Accessibility to Basic Needs

Drinkable water and breathable air: these are two things we cannot live without and cannot take for granted. Some of our fellow humans in different parts of this world have only one, or neither. Look no further than the beautiful and amazing country of India. The people of India touch most of our lives daily, though we do not even realize it.

The people of India have contributed significantly to various fields all over the world.

- **Technology:** Indian professionals and entrepreneurs have made significant contributions to the technology industry. Indian-origin CEOs lead major companies like Google, Microsoft, and IBM. Additionally, Indian engineers and developers are highly sought after in Silicon Valley and have played a key role in the development of many innovative products and services.
- **Healthcare:** Indian doctors and healthcare professionals are in high demand around the world, especially in developed countries where there is a shortage of skilled medical personnel. Many Indian doctors have made significant contributions to medical research and innovation as well.
- **Education:** Indian academics and scholars have made notable contributions to various fields of study, including science, literature, and philosophy. Indian universities have also produced some of the world's most distinguished scholars and scientists.
- **Business:** Indian entrepreneurs have built successful businesses around the world, creating jobs and contributing to the economies

of various countries. Many Indian businesses are known for their innovation and ability to adapt to changing markets.

- **Arts and culture:** Indian artists, musicians, and filmmakers have made significant contributions to the arts and entertainment industries around the world. Indian cinema, for example, is widely popular and has had a significant impact on global culture.

To put it lightly, the people of India have made significant contributions in various fields and have played an important role in shaping the global economy, culture, and society.

Despite these monumental contributions to humankind, the demand for water in India will soon significantly outpace supply. Dr. Yogesh Simmhan is working with EqWater, using data analytics and machine learning to understand differences in access to water for individual neighborhoods. The idea is that algorithms can be used to better manage supplies, such as improved water scheduling or detecting leaks.[12]

According to Engineer Bainomugisha, 9 out of 10 people in the world breathe unhealthy air each day, adversely affecting lower-income countries and individuals.[13] Whether it is he and his team working to detect pollution to help infirm communities on how to lessen exposure and prevent further pollution or the University of Houston's Air Quality Forecasting and Modeling Lab's model that can predict ozone pollution up to 14 days ahead of time,[14] AI's use in the area of pollution is growing every day.

Unlocking Value with AI for Economic and Social Mobility

As the wealth gap continues to widen and poverty is still unsolved, we see the devastating effects on the impoverished nations and people of the world. How can we unleash AI to combat this seemingly irreversible inequity?

The McKinsey Global Institute has run simulations on what the impact of AI could be on the global economy. Two of their more interesting findings are:

1. There is large potential for AI to contribute to global economic activity, potentially delivering an additional $13 trillion of global economic activity by 2030, an additional 1.2 percent GDP growth per year.

2. A key challenge is that adoption of AI could widen gaps among countries, companies, and workers.[15]

All counties and enterprises must adapt and install AI whenever and wherever they can. Those who fail could see leading AI countries capture an additional 20 to 25 percent in net economic benefit, with developing countries only about 5 to 15 percent.

The social safety nets across the globe are another area in which AI could benefit the impoverished and less fortunate. The argument has been presented of AI's ability to radically improve the efficiency and quality of public service delivery in education, healthcare, and social protection. Successful pilots include automation of Sweden's social services and the government of Togo's experimenting with machine learning using mobile phone metadata and satellite images to identify households most in need of social assistance.[16]

Expert Input and Analysis: How LG Is Improving Quality of Life Through Innovation

By Dr. Sokwoo Rhee, Corporate Senior Vice President at LG Electronics and Head of the LG North America Innovation Center

LG NOVA, the North America Innovation Center for LG Electronics, launched the Mission for the Future program in 2021. The program is a global initiative to bring in outside companies of all sizes and stages to LG to explore business collaboration and broaden our ability to innovate and expand in areas that are new to LG. Through this program, we've invited companies, startups, and entrepreneurs to propose their social impact business ideas for the opportunity to grow and work with LG.

The founding of the LG NOVA program and the challenge lean into LG Electronics' brand mission of Innovation for a Better Life. LG NOVA builds on this in its passion for improving the quality of life through technology and its belief that anything is possible through innovation.

(continued)

We recognize that innovation comes from everywhere and we can be even more innovative as a company if we collaborate with others outside of LG in the community where they are building solutions from the ground up. We're looking to harness this creative brain power to create really impactful solutions.

The power of creative collaboration, strategic partnership, and community-focus effort will continue to spark ideation that will improve quality of life, creating a smarter, healthier, more-connected future. These partnerships—powered in most cases by machine learning and AI—drive change in myriad industries like digital healthcare, electric mobility, and more, bolstered by technology that is making an impact globally.

At the end of the day, we hope to deliver innovations for smarter living, climate change, sustainability, and digital health—some of the most pressing challenges and goals of today. The LG NOVA program is unique in the sense that we are looking for transformative change. By dedicating time, resources, and capital in these partnerships we can bring revolutionary concepts to life and mass markets faster.

For example, by working with startups in the electric mobility/EV space, such as SparkCharge, a grid-free EV charging solution company and a finalist in the first annual Mission for the Future challenge announced in September 2022, LG is helping to build up the infrastructure needed to support a future of widespread EV adoption that will impact sustainability and climate change.

For digital health, LG is working with startups such as XRHealth, a virtual treatment room developer and another finalist from the first annual Mission for the Future challenge, that makes healthcare more accessible at the home and hospital level.

That's why we engage with companies in North America and across the globe that are creating solutions to deliver the future of sustainable, readily accessible, socially impactful, and technologically advanced living for society at large.

The responsibility of uncovering new business opportunities built to benefit people, communities, and the planet

LG Electronics is built on the core principle of making life better for people and the planet. At the corporate level, we've made commitments to sustainable business strategies, carbon reduction, and renewable energy initiatives. We also build high-quality products that support people in their homes and give them a better life.

Our efforts at LG NOVA are a natural extension of this commitment. Through LG NOVA's work, we're taking an active role in innovating to create a positive future for all. This vision has been brought to life over the past two years through our Mission for the Future program. The program is a way for us to get ahead of the innovation cycle and grow companies that we believe will play a role in getting us to the future faster with positive benefits for us all.

Future growth, business opportunities, and revenue are all in alignment. LG chooses to lead and grow the company around how it can better serve people and the planet, as a way toward growth and revenue.

Implementation and leveraging AI technology to accelerate the positive impact LG's work has on society and the planet

AI is one of the most advanced tools in technology that is constantly growing and resulting in new business opportunities and use cases. Especially in the startup world, AI is resulting in exponential growth of new market areas in technology, across all sectors. We're seeing companies create novel cutting-edge applications in the metaverse, smart life, healthcare, and more. Backed by startups, AI algorithms can enable hospitals to better analyze data and diagnose patients, offer advances in self-driving cars, and improve supply chain efficiency.

For example, HealthSnap, part of the 2022 Mission for the Future selection cohort, is an integrated virtual care management platform

(continued)

that uses AI-guided care coordination, remote patient monitoring, chronic care management, and more. This company works with a number of healthcare providers, one provider noting that the company improves the quality and cost of care by offering a sustainable method of viewing and responding to patient health data, leveraging data to predict and react to events before they happen.

Another example is IEMS Solution, also a finalist for the Mission for the Future challenge in 2022. This startup leverages innovative AI and blockchain-based distributed energy resources management systems (DERMS) and transactive energy software platforms, enabling optimization across e-mobility solutions, smart cities, and homes. Its software solutions help EV-fleet operators plan and operate their systems with minimum cost with the maximum reliability and resiliency—changing the landscape of the future of mobility. Companies like these will only continue to accelerate uses of AI and creative solutions, elevating technology for years to come.

PART

II | Digital Transformation and Society

The United Nations recently released the results of the "2022 E-Government Survey" (https://publicadministration.un.org/en/Research/UN-e-Government-Surveys), which shows progress, surprises, and opportunity for governments across the globe in their shift to the digitization of services. COVID-19 has accelerated the need for governments to become more and more digitally accessible for their citizens as an increasing percentage of people became more digitally savvy during the pandemic. Meeting your customers (in this case, your citizens) where they are, instead of forcing them to do things your way, is always the wise way to do business. But, moving the enormous bureaucratic icebergs that are governments is complicated, messy, and sometimes near impossible.

As governments worldwide are looking to streamline the delivery of services through mobile, cloud, automation, and digitization processes, what will the future of person-to-government interaction look like? Will our relationships with our governmental entities become "better"? Or, will the archaic technologies that governments have invested in previously become a hindrance to actual progress?

In Chapters 3 through 5, we cover the future of work, digital disruption, and technologies that are driving society's digital transformation.

3

The Future of Work

You may ask, what is meant by "the future of work"? The future of work is merely a prediction of how the work being done, the workplace, and the labor force will progress and evolve in the years to come. Why is it important that CEOs and other C-suite executives accurately forecast these future changes? Why is it imperative that they understand how that evolution will affect the following?

- What work is being done?
- What technology is needed to do the work?
- Who is doing the work?
- What skills are required to do the work?
- When and from where is the work being done?

C-suite executives of organizations worldwide will make calculated decisions about future workforce planning, based upon their current knowledge and what they anticipate the work world of the future will look like. As a result, HR experts and management must educate themselves about how their workplace will be impacted in the future.

We answer these questions and share important skill sets and jobs we can expect to see develop in the next 10 years. We also discuss how these changes will affect the future customer experience (CX) and how artificial intelligence will alter human creativity and experiences.

Evolving Work Trends

While much focus is placed on technology in future-of-work discussions, other factors, such as remote employment and the gig economy, play a large role in not only how work will be done, but who will be doing it and from where. In addition, employers will want to consider what the work is, as a 2020 research report from the Society for Human Resource Management and Willis Towers Watson noted that "85 percent of jobs that will exist in 2030 have not been invented yet."[1]

ChatGPT and Jobs of the Future

According to Goldman Sachs, ChatGPT is poised to disrupt every major industry and potentially replace over 300 million jobs. While this technology has the potential to increase global GDP by 7% within the next decade, many individuals may struggle to comprehend and adapt to its impact.[2]

The transformative power of generative AI extends to every aspect of society, including industry, government, and various fields such as software engineering, journalism, and scientific research. It is anticipated that this technology will fundamentally alter business processes in a manner not seen since the advent of the Internet.

However, this development is not without its societal implications, particularly in regard to employment. Translators, public relations professionals, writers, journalists, authors, accountants, auditors, scientists, and many other professions are likely to experience significant changes in the wake of this technological revolution.

Goldman Sachs has projected that approximately 7% of workers may lose their jobs entirely within the next decade, with this figure potentially rising to 50% of companies impacted. However, the organization suggests that affected individuals will likely find alternative employment opportunities, although the specifics of these opportunities remain uncertain.

Furthermore, Goldman Sachs states that the implementation of generative AI could result in a 1.5% increase in US labor productivity, which is double the current rate and has significant implications. Additionally, AI growth could result in a 1.4% increase in global GDP, representing an additional $6 trillion annually over 10 years.

What Jobs Will Cease to Exist?   The potential impact of generative AI on various industries and professions is a critical question. Will creative and white-collar jobs become obsolete, and how will research be affected? Many companies are now investing in this technology, including Open AI, and competition in this field is rapidly increasing.

Nevertheless, it is anticipated that jobs related to content, marketing, and public relations may be most vulnerable to disruption. The precise impact of generative AI on the labor market and economy is yet to be fully understood, and further research and analysis are required.

The rapid development of AI tools has led to their increasing sophistication, allowing them to perform routine tasks that were traditionally the domain of interpreters, writers, and auditors. This trend is gaining momentum, and we are witnessing the beginning of the era of large language models, which are likely to evolve rapidly in the coming weeks and months.

While some may argue that the focus of this development is on improving productivity and efficiency, the impact of automation on jobs cannot be ignored. It is clear that automation will have a significant impact on productivity, efficiency, and speed in the workplace, but it will also have implications for the workforce as a whole.

Human Intervention Is Essential   In order to create these advanced AI tools and frameworks, human intervention is essential. Therefore, there will be an increased demand for individuals with specialized skills in AI creation and engineering. It is important to note that while there may be concerns that these developments could lead to widespread job losses, history has shown that new technologies often create new job opportunities, and it is likely that this will be the case with the evolution of AI.

While automation may transform certain job roles and tasks, it is unlikely to replace all jobs entirely. Additionally, the continued evolution of AI technology presents numerous possibilities for innovative solutions that can benefit the workforce and the economy as a whole.

It is evident that AI tools are becoming increasingly sophisticated and are able to handle routine tasks that were previously the responsibility of interpreters, writers, and auditors. We are witnessing the emergence of large language or foundation models, which is just the beginning of a rapidly evolving trend. The impact of this development will be felt across all industries and professions, and while some may argue that it will only serve to enhance productivity and efficiency, there is no doubt that automation will play a significant role in the future.

The automation of tasks will undoubtedly lead to an increase in productivity and efficiency, and will ultimately enable us to achieve our goals at a faster pace. While the fear of job losses due to technological advancements is not new, history has shown that new technologies often create new and different jobs. The emergence of automation engineering, for example, is a potential outcome of this development.

While some jobs will be transformed, there is a likelihood that professional jobs will be reskilled and adapted to leverage AI capabilities, leading to improved productivity and enhanced job roles. For example, anecdotal evidence has shown that certain AI tools, such as ChatGPT, could pass medical school exams and coding interviews. However, wider adoption is necessary to gauge the potential impact of AI on jobs and human beings in the enterprise world.

Governmental Oversight and Potential Biases   There are some concerns that need to be addressed by the government and companies regarding the use of AI in general. One such concern is the potential for bias and the production of misinformation. Additionally, AI technologies increase the risk of misleading images and text. To mitigate these risks, human judgment and review will become increasingly important.

Many jobs are expected to undergo profound transformation, with some being more heavily impacted than others. For example, communication and media jobs, such as advertising, copyediting, and journalism, are likely to be one of the initial professions to feel the impact. AI technology has been trained to analyze massive amounts of encyclopedic or textual data, making it ideal for these industries. While AI components and technologies could help with tasks such as scriptwriting and brainstorming, human judgment and review will remain critical to ensure accuracy and eliminate bias.

While some remedial work may be phased out, complete replacement is not feasible. Conversational AI and natural language processing (NLP) are already making strides in customer service, and chatbots are taking over some tasks for customers. However, customers expect natural conversations on complex topics, and this requires both deterministic conversational AI agents and chat GPT to provide human-like conversation and usefulness.

By raising the bar, humans can provide higher value and retention, especially for complex cases.

Software engineering is already changing with the advent of low-code and no-code platforms, where objects generate much of the code. However, manual coding still dominates, and automation is lacking, which slows down the agility process. Generative AI technologies, such as GPT, could speed up the generation and optimization of code, reducing the manual coding process, improving sustainability and efficiency, and providing engineers and managers with more tools for optimization. This could lead to greater productivity, but it will also mean that many jobs will undergo significant changes. Enterprises and governments must work in concert to guide this evolution so it does not adversely affect one segment of society.

Generative AI and Enhanced Job Market Efficiency   Lastly, I would like to address the idea proposed by Goldman Sachs regarding how generative AI could enhance job market efficiency. It is true that AI has the potential to produce a massive amount of data insights leading to better profitability and opportunities, but it comes with a cost.

Currently, we are witnessing the integration of AI in personalized customer experiences, customer support, and task automation, with potential expansion into new industries and opportunities. However, this also means that new jobs will be created not only in technology but also in other areas.

If AI is positioned correctly, it has the potential to promote diversity and inclusion in the market. To achieve this, we need to take measures to identify biases and remove them when hiring, ensuring unbiased and equal protection to candidates. Innovation and growth can occur if we implement AI correctly, revolutionizing opportunities, inclusiveness, and transforming our society. Generative AI, in particular, can be a powerful tool in unlocking human creativity and capabilities.

How Will the Work Be Done?

The use of technology has provided opportunities for companies to transform their business practices. For instance, companies such as Uber and Amazon have embraced the platform and marketplace models, whereas Airbnb has effectively utilized the sharing economy. As a result, our traditional views on work, which typically focus on individual jobs, have been challenged.

"Successful organizations are shifting their thinking toward the capabilities needed to win in their marketplace. Through strategic modeling of future workforce options, they clarify the future roles, skills, and mindsets to deliver their strategy. They then focus on sourcing and developing these through reskilling, upskilling, recruitment or drawing on the wider 'gig economy' of flexible workers."[3]

When and Where Will the Work Be Done?

One work trend involves where and when future work will be done. The advent of COVID-19 and the resulting coronavirus pandemic cast a spotlight on just how many jobs in the workplace can successfully be done remotely. The pandemic accelerated this transition from working in-office to working predominantly from home. But the shift toward organizations allowing more employees, in a broader range of professions, the ability to choose between working remotely, in the office, or a combination of the two (hybrid), has been increasing since the late 1990s.

> More employees will work from home. . . . A large majority—82 percent—of executives say they intend to let employees work remotely at least part of the time, according to a survey by Gartner Inc., a Stamford, Conn.-based research, and advisory firm. Nearly half—47 percent—say they will allow employees to work remotely full time.[4]

In addition, employee data collection will expand. Hybrid work has fostered greater interest in monitoring workplace productivity and employee wellness. Gartner analysis shows that 16% of employers are more frequently using technologies to monitor their employees.

By monitoring employee activity, companies can identify areas where employees may be wasting time or not using their time effectively, and take steps to improve their work processes.

Another reason to monitor employee activity is to ensure compliance with company policies and regulations. For example, companies may need to monitor employees to ensure that they are not engaging in unethical or illegal behavior, such as sharing confidential information or engaging in discriminatory practices.

In addition, some companies may use monitoring technology to assess employee performance and provide feedback for improvement. This can be useful in identifying areas in which additional training or support may be needed.

Overall, the use of technology to monitor employee work can help companies improve productivity, ensure compliance with policies and regulations, and provide feedback to employees for professional development. However, it is important for companies to balance the benefits of monitoring with the potential privacy concerns of their employees, and to ensure that any monitoring practices are transparent and fair.

Specific Changes in the Workplace

A number of the concepts, patterns, and actions that will influence the future of work in 2030 can already be observed in the present. Nonetheless, certain changes are taking shape more discreetly, and it's possible that corporate executives may not fully comprehend their implications for enhancing performance, boosting productivity, and retaining skilled personnel.

A study performed by Coldwell Banker Richard Ellis (CBRE), the world's largest commercial real estate services and investment firm, and Genesis Equity Partners, LLC, a real estate developer associated with a company in Western China, interviewed 220 global experts, office workers, and young people in North America, Europe, and the Asia Pacific.

According to their research:

> . . . many of the ideas, trends and behaviors that will shape work in 2030 are already evident today. However, some of these changes are quietly emerging and business leaders might not truly understand the significance of their impact on performance, productivity, and retaining talent.[5]

Based on this study, in the next 10 years:

- We will exchange "workplaces" for "places to work." These places to work will have a variety of different quiet areas, rooms, and offices to give workers a choice of where they would like to work. The study predicted that "mood-based work" areas and "no assigned seating" will also be a trend. This allows employees to select a place to work based on their mood, their need for focus or concentration, and how they feel each day.

- Collaboration at work will take place at round tables and circular layouts.
- Organizations will be smaller and specialize their products and services to stand out from the majority.
- There will be less hierarchy, more teams, and "everyone" will be a leader. "For decades leadership has been seen in hierarchical terms—rising to the top of the "pipeline" that results in Executive Leadership . . . Executive Leadership needs to shift to "Enterprise Leadership."[6]
- Offices will place more emphasis on wellness, offering healthier environments such as sleeping rooms, relaxation areas, art, music, and allowing pets at work. "Workers will demand better treatment for themselves and their communities from their employers."[7]
- "Organizations will re-examine how they impact the environment. . . . Going forward, chief sustainability officers will be expected to look at their company's environmental impact on workers, suppliers, customers, and communities."[8]
- A new C-suite role will emerge, the "chief of work." This new role will establish and direct the culture within the organization, drive the employee work experience, and perhaps even decide the type of work environment and technology that is used.

Additional adjustments to where and when work is currently done versus where and when it will be done in the future are:

- As geographic and technological limitations fade away, the workforce will become more widely distributed.
- The standard 9-to-5 workday will move to a more fluid structure as work is done at any time, and from anywhere in the world.

"[These] trends may seem simple, but truly understanding the metrics behind these ideas is needed for business success. Only forward-thinking organizations who take the time to understand and explore these metrics now will know what's needed for a productive, collaborative, successful, workplace [or, shall we say, place to work] of the future.[9]

Expert Input and Analysis: AI and Social Contract Perspective

by James Hodson, Chief Executive Officer of AI for Good Foundation
Blueprint for an AI-Enabled Society

In the 1870s, and through the early years of the twentieth century, electricity was considered a mysterious force with almost magical powers, and deadly strength. Over the course of the twentieth century, electrification of cities, our homes, and our lives dramatically changed our societies and economies. Electricity accelerated urbanization, economic development, and supported major leaps forward in healthcare, education, and humans' overall quality of life and access to opportunity. However, where the lack of access to electrified infrastructure still persists, the levels of economic inequality have been magnified. Electricity also shifted the centers of economic development, and caused structural changes in employment—devastating large industries that were no longer viable once electricity was widely available (e.g. gas lamp operators).

It is inviting to observe parallels between electrification (the Second Industrial Revolution) and artificial intelligence (the nth Industrial Revolution, depending on who is counting). In their purest theoretical form, artificially intelligent systems will without a doubt be able to reproduce most or all human behaviors, skills, and adaptations. There will be a point where humanoid systems may be engineered to be practically indistinguishable in daily interactions, and significantly lower the cost of labor for economic production that relies on complex manual tasks, collaborative tasks, and physical manipulation of the environment. There will be a point when almost any task comprising intellectual logical operations may be completed faster via machine, and more effectively incorporate available information and constraints. Our most well-engineered machines will be able to produce more accurate output, faster, and more reliably than most human beings, most of the time. This will not lead to a "singularity" or "runaway intelligence," but it will lead to an incredible wealth of scientific and technological opportunity, with more efficient pathways

(continued)

to realization than we have experienced before—the laws of physics, conservation of energy, and finance, will likely remain unperturbed.

Our empirical work in artificial intelligence research is beginning to approach some of the central questions that would enable the theoretical capabilities mentioned above. But society will not change overnight, job markets will not collapse from one day to the next, and we still may guide social development and economic development toward outcomes that are Pareto optimal—doing the most good for the largest number of people.

So, what will likely happen?

As the means to production become cheaper and more readily accessible to enterprising individuals and organizations, we will likely see a medium-term boost in market competitiveness, with the few companies well-capitalized enough to maintain state-of-the-art models becoming marketplaces and de-facto operating systems for new capabilities. The cost of energy will remain the largest friction limiting progress in the short term, which will soon be replaced by diminishing returns from larger models, and the need to look for substantially different methods for new sources of improvements and energy efficiency. This transition will likely cool the exuberance and expectations seen between 2019 and 2023, and provide a natural period of economic adaptation and proof of value for new capabilities.

From the perspective of industry, investment in artificial intelligence-facing capabilities will continue to increase, which will lead to increased labor demand across many sectors. This increased demand will be seen across the entire constellation of bringing new products and capabilities to market. The primary decrease in labor inputs will at first be seen in areas with historical offshoring practices—including call centers, outsourced software development, and outsourced content generation and management. We will likely experience a contraction of globalized workforces as it becomes cost-effective to bring capabilities back onto US soil. This trend will be accelerated as intelligent capabilities continue to be incorporated into modern manufacturing facilities, and as capital allocation cycles start to align for large-scale infrastructure investments.

The creative industries will see increased competition due to a drop in professional production costs from automation and assistive technologies. Demand is unlikely to significantly change, which will lead to the fragmentation of such markets and the integration of creative processes into vertically-aligned business processes in other industries, where physical products sustain the organization. Larger infrastructure-oriented companies will also become more prone to competitive pressures and innovation-led disruption, creating pathways to increased adoption of new capabilities through more nimble and smaller networks of economic cooperation and companies.

What will society look like?

The important constraint will remain demand—consumption will not dramatically increase, which means innovation will cater more and more to those markets where consumers can be influenced on shorter time horizons. The engine of economic productivity will become more project-focused than company-focused.

Inevitably, such a shift in economic structure will change the nature of employment. Companies will find it more difficult to hire full-time employees over extended time horizons, and human labor will likely prefer to move to where it is needed most at a particular point in time, and where the opportunities lie. The United States saw enormous growth of the so-called "gig economy" between 2010 and 2020, and the model is likely to spread further. This means that we will no longer be able to rely on companies as the central construct of stability in people's lives, nor the central construct for distribution of economic value. Instead, it is likely that we will look to balance the taxation of economic value creation with the incentives necessary to maintain growth on acceptable terms, and not unnecessarily reduce economic participation. This also means rewarding people for social labor that is uncompensated by its nature, but is necessary to the success of the system overall (such as family-based caregivers).

It is no less certain that we will need to provide access to a choice of supporting structures that enable people control over their nutrition, education, health, housing, and basic living needs. Governance structures have historically lagged heavily behind private industry in

(continued)

technology adoption and innovation, with digital government services still in their infancy in most advanced economies as of 2023. However, accessibility and inclusivity of digital supporting structures (and the role AI can play in this) will play a central role in determining the extent to which social equity can be achieved over the medium to long term. We must find ways to do this without undermining people's autonomy and participation in democratic institutions, and we must enable transparency and accountability so that any centralization or monopolization of resources can be addressed to keep markets operating efficiently.

Beyond our borders, we have a duty to ensure that the benefits of increasingly sophisticated artificial intelligence technologies will become available to all. That means working with marginalized communities and in less economically developed countries to ensure that technology can enhance political and economic stability, and that technology capabilities reflect the linguistic and cultural needs of diverse groups. The largest danger from artificial intelligence will not be from a hostile breed of machines due to exponential growth in intelligence, but from exacerbation of enormous existing inequalities through exponential growth in the digital divide.

Who Will Do the Work?

There will be a need for traditional full-time and part-time workers as well as gig economy workers (short-term contract and freelance workers), and employees supplied by staffing organizations.

Leading global learning company Pearson researched what employment might look like in 2030. They predict the following:

- Just one in five workers today will be in a similar role in the future.
- In 10 years' time, 50% of jobs will be changed by automation—but only 5% will be eliminated.[10]
- Professions associated with agriculture, construction, and trades, which have been projected to decrease in other similar studies, may offer areas of opportunity for certain skill sets.

- Only 1 in 10 workers in the education and healthcare sectors are in careers that are expected to grow.
- Seven out of 10 workers hold jobs that have an uncertain future.
- "Technology's rapid transformation will continue, forcing companies to rethink how to integrate people with machines. . . . The increased use of technology will eliminate jobs. That means companies will need to reskill employees to prepare them for new tasks and responsibilities."[11]

These findings and others like them emphasize how important it is that HR does their part to prepare the current workforce for future new career paths. Upskilling and digital dexterity will outweigh tenure and experience. HR will have to establish and promote a continuous learning environment, meaning that knowledge acquisition and transparency across the organization must become a part of day-to-day operations.

It is important that business leaders analyze existing roles, provide advanced training, and offer employees opportunities to learn entirely new skillsets. Otherwise, the worker of the future will not only be unemployed, but they may very well be unemployable.

Skills of the Future

The future of work is very much on the shoulders of the worker. They have to grab hold and create their own careers. They cannot simply sit back and let their careers happen to them. In order to pursue new job opportunities or adapt to changes in their current roles, workers will need to acquire new skills. However, despite concerns about automation, some business leaders are not adequately preparing their employees with the necessary skills. While almost half of business leaders (45%) acknowledge automation initiatives and demonstrate awareness of the situation, only a small percentage (15%) communicate about upskilling initiatives. This lack of attention to upskilling is likely to result in a significant mismatch between workers and job requirements in the future. It is projected that 9 out of 10 jobs will require digital skills, yet currently, 44% of Europeans aged 16–74 lack even basic digital abilities. In Europe, this skills gap is expected to lead to approximately 1.67 million unfilled vacancies for ICT professionals by 2025.[12]

Pearson states that, in the United States, ". . . there is a particularly strong emphasis on interpersonal skills. These skills include teaching, social perceptiveness, and coordination, as well as related knowledge, such as psychology and anthropology. . . . Our findings also confirm the importance of higher-order cognitive skills such as . . ."[13] those that will be most in demand in the future; for example:

- Complex problem solving
- Originality
- Active learning
- Fluency of ideas

A report from the McKinsey Global Institute states that "Automation and AI will accelerate the shift in skills that the workforce needs . . ."[14] and also predicts a dramatic increase in demand for more employee hours across the other three skill sets, which are:

- **Higher cognitive:** These skills include advanced literacy and writing, quantitative and statistical skills, critical thinking, and complex information processing. Doctors, accountants, research analysts, writers, and editors typically use these.
- **Social and emotional:** Or so-called "soft skills," these include advanced communication and negotiation, empathy, the ability to learn continuously, to manage others, and to be adaptable. Business development, programming, emergency response, and counseling require these skills.
- **Technological:** This embraces everything from basic to advanced IT skills, data analysis, engineering, and research. These are skills that are likely to be the most highly rewarded as companies seek more software developers, engineers, robotics, and scientific experts.[15]

Pearson went on to explain, "A similar picture emerges for the U.K. The results point to a particularly strong relationship between higher-order cognitive skills and future occupational demand. Skills related to":[16]

- System thinking
- The ability to recognize, understand, and act on interconnections and feedback loops in sociotechnical systems

- Judgment and decision making
- Systems analysis
- Systems evaluation

Pearson went on to relate that in addition to the more specialized features needed for specific professions, the future workforce will also need broad-based knowledge.

Research suggests that the work of the future will witness a shift away from low-skill occupations such as machine operators, cashiers, typists, and other office support and toward technology professionals such as information communication technology (ICT) specialists, network architects, systems analysts, and computer engineers.

The shift away from low-skill occupations toward technology professionals can be beneficial to people for several reasons. First, technology jobs typically require higher education and specialized skills, which can lead to higher wages and better job security compared to low-skill occupations that are more likely to be automated. This can help workers achieve greater financial stability and upward mobility.

Second, technology jobs are often seen as more creative and intellectually stimulating, providing workers with greater job satisfaction and a sense of purpose. This can lead to greater job engagement and motivation, which can positively impact mental health and well-being.

Third, as technology continues to advance and become more integrated into our daily lives, the demand for skilled technology professionals is expected to increase. This means that workers who have the necessary skills and education in technology may have a greater variety of job opportunities available to them.

Overall, the shift toward technology professions can provide individuals with greater financial stability, job satisfaction, and a wider range of job opportunities. However, it is important to ensure that workers have access to the necessary education and training to acquire the skills needed to succeed in these fields.

Jobs of the Future

Over the next 10 years, 1.2 billion employees worldwide will be affected by the adaptation of automation technologies and AI. This is equal to 50% of the world economy and will disrupt US$14.6 trillion in wages.

It is important to note that while automation will change 50 percent of jobs, it is not expected to eliminate more than 5 percent. Rather than being replaced by computers, most workers will instead work alongside rapidly evolving machines. The future of work will see a shift in demand away from office support positions, machine operators, and other low-skill professions—and toward technology professionals such as computer engineers and information communication technology (ICT) specialists.[17]

The team from Fast Future wrote a report for the UK government on *The Shape of Jobs to Come*. In their study they pointed out new job titles and responsibilities that might appear on the world scene by the year 2030. Five of the 20 new job titles Fast Future thinks will materialize

as a result of exponential developments and breakthroughs in science and technology are:

1. **Life Manager for the Techno-Bewildered**—Those who struggle with technology and get left behind in the new world order might find themselves placed under the mentorship of new-age social workers. These Life Managers would supervise our every decision, guide us on how to navigate the day-to-day of a tech-centric world, and help ensure we use our finances or guaranteed basic incomes in a sustainable manner.

2. **Robo-Nanny**—Replacing the human nanny or au pair, future robotic caregivers could become a constant companion to our children at every stage of their development. Every facet of a Robo-Nanny's character could be selected and tweaked by parents—emotional intelligence, values, ethics, levels of optimism, and even how the bot responds to difficult situations such as the passing of a grandparent. The bot could also be programmed to introduce new learning topics, languages, and life skills as required.

3. **End of Life Planner/Death Strategist**—As lifespans are extended for those who can afford it, deciding when to die becomes a difficult decision. Our choices will need to factor in emotional, healthcare, familial, economic, and tax planning criteria when making the decisions. This will give rise to a new death management profession—part GP, part financial advisor, part family therapist, and part grief counselor.

4. **Independent Fact Checker**—This role already exists to some extent but becomes evermore essential as concerns grow over the proliferation of fake news, companies exaggerating their marketing claims, and politicians arguing about the veracity of each other's statements. These arbiters of truth will use a swath of AI systems to check the truth and origin of every claim and fact. Clients will pay them for these services and for a regularly updated assessment of how truthful and accurate their own statements are. Public honesty tables provided by the fact checkers will influence the reputations and fortunes of businesses, politicians, and political parties.

5. **Robot Whisperers**—Artificially intelligent robots may comprise a significant part of the future workforce in retail, food service, and hospitality. Companies deploying such robots may require a staff of professional human Robot Whisperers to stand guard whenever the bots interact with the public. This job would involve behind-the-scenes monitoring of robotic chefs and customer service robots to make sure they don't run over a person's foot or knock over a gas grill or cause other such hazards. The Whisperer would also monitor for undesirable behavioral changes as the robots learn from and adapt to their environment. Although robotic employees could be highly efficient and autonomous, it is possible that unexpected stimuli in the environment could result in accidents or injuries. Robot Whisperers would be a profession geared toward instilling public trust in robot workers.

6. **Inter-AI Conflict Resolution Specialist**—AIs will increasingly need to collaborate. Our personal intelligent assistant may need to interact with the AIs of our bank, our employers, and all the vendors who serve us. Not all AIs will be born equal or have common goals, so disputes could arise. Human arbitrators may need to intervene to get the best outcome for humanity in these disputes.

7. **Robo-Cop Coordinator**—With the increasing capability of AI and robotics, policing could be undertaken by automated robotic systems. These might range from humanoid robots capable of interacting directly with the public, through to autonomous road vehicles and drones for surveillance. Human oversight would enable resources to be deployed based on the recommendations made by automated systems given the situation observed. The coordinators would be able to supervise a significant number of policing assets, all of which would be capable of operating 24/7.

8. **Autonomous Vehicle Ethicist**—We will need to establish the guiding principles for decisions made by autonomous vehicles. For example, who or what should the car hit if an accident is inevitable? Depending on where you are in the world the decision will be governed by different ethical and religious considerations, societal norms, and even economic factors.

9. **Human Enhancement Technician**—As a society, we are starting to augment the human body with chemical, genetic, electronic, and physical enhancements. Body shops will appear on the high street where appropriately trained technicians will be able to perform these upgrades—administering nootropic drugs, genetic modifications, 3D printed limbs, and electronic brain stimulation.

10. **Chief Augmentation Officer (CAO)**—Within a decade, an increasing number of staff members could be seeking bodily augmentations that render them close to superhuman cyborgs. These humans 2.0 may need to have different management, working conditions, and workplace rights—all designed and overseen by the CAO.[18]

Are we really ready for the jobs of tomorrow? When we consider many of these potential occupations of the future, they may appear to be too big of a stretch for the imagination. Nevertheless, in each instance, significant advances in present-day society are taking place in the essential disciplines of science and technology. These developments imply that many of these jobs will become a reality in the decades to come. We ask the question once more, are the public in general, our schooling, and systems of higher education prepared?

Human Capital Development

During the pandemic, many office workers and those in technology were able to easily transition to working at home if they had Internet access. We found that many lower-skilled workers did not have that option and were required to be physically present on their jobs, many of whom worked in the manufacturing, retail, and public transportation sectors. The COVID-19 crisis has only increased concerns regarding the quality and permanence of some occupations.

56% of the Work Will Be Done Digitally by 2025

Ten years out, the picture is expected to be quite different as Industry 4.0 technologies like AI and the IoT become commonplace. According to a McKinsey study cited by [Cile Montgomery, a senior consultant with Dell Technologies Unified Workspace], "60 percent of jobs will be transformed through the automation of component tasks by 2030."[19]

Mobile technology and cloud-based solutions have made the notion of working anywhere in the world, any time of the day or night, a reality. Work is becoming much less a place that you go to and more a set of tasks and duties that one performs.

The Rise of the Digital Platform and Extended Ecosystems: By 2025, driven by volatile global conditions, 75% of business leaders will leverage digital platforms and ecosystem capabilities to adapt their value chains to new markets, industries, and ecosystems.

Accelerating Digital Experiences: By 2022, 70% of all organizations will have accelerated use of digital technologies, transforming existing business processes to drive customer engagement, employee productivity, and business resiliency.

In its IT Spending and Staffing Benchmarks 2021/22 report, market research firm Computer Economics described technology's role in the rapid recovery from the pandemic as "nothing short of a miracle." Digital transformation passed the test, it seems. Going forward, Computer Economics suggested that the "low-hanging fruit" in cloud migration is now picked and that "We are now in the stage of digital transformation where we are not just replacing existing tools—we are now enhancing them."[20]

Nearly 14 percent of jobs in OECD countries are likely to be automated, while another 32 percent are at high risk of being partially automated. Young people and those with low skills are those at highest risk—but new technological developments are now also affecting the jobs of the highly skilled too.[21]

The question that must be answered is, are lower-skilled workers and those most vulnerable to job loss receiving the training they so desperately need? Governments and corporations will have to investigate the best ways to help people gain the skills they will need in the ever-changing world of work.

July 2021 saw the highest ever share of US employers with unfilled positions. 50% of all employees will need reskilling by 2025. 74% of professionals believe employee turnover will only increase in the coming year. With employers no longer able to rely on a steady source of external talent, internal mobility becomes more important than ever. Not only can it help fill talent gaps, especially for niche roles—it can also prevent attrition by providing employees with opportunities to learn, develop and grow.[22]

Expert Input and Analysis: How Genpact Leverages Technology for Critical Challenges to Humanity

By Tiger Tyagarajan, President and Chief Executive Officer, Genpact

In recent years business leaders are becoming far more cognizant of the impact of business on the environment with the ongoing challenges we are all facing with climate change.

Addressing climate change should just be the start. For companies that are losing interest in environment, social, and governance issues (let's all admit that there's a growing backlash), now is the time to double down on ESG programs. Governance has always been important, but environmental and social are fundamentally long-term risks to businesses that need to be managed.

We're in a meaningful position to help our clients achieve progress on their ESG agendas through areas like supply chain optimization, climate footprint of equipment usage, sustainable procurement, community safety, anti-money laundering, data management, and ESG reporting, among other areas.

What's more, as sustainability initiatives drive greater competitive advantage, innovation, and financial performance, sustainability investments will continue to grow. Companies that make the right bets today will be the winners in the long term.

We believe that climate change is not only an existential issue of our time, but it is also a massive data and change management problem. The three main steps to using technology and data for action and social impact are as follows:

- **Define industry-specific goals:** It's critical to take an industry-led approach. Enterprises should lay out sustainability objectives that are right for their business and industry to achieve the most significant results.
- **Build a framework:** When you identify sustainability goals, you can use data to guide your action plan. With technologies like machine learning and AI, enterprises can rely on data modeling and forecasting techniques to analyze how current processes connect with sustainability goals, such as reducing energy consumption.
- **Combine human and machine intelligence:** Success is not just about having the best and latest technology to drive sustainability goals. Human expertise is still critical, which is where augmented intelligence comes in. In essence, artificial intelligence takes over many data processing tasks, unlocking insights at speed so that teams can make confident data-driven decisions.

By following these steps, companies can address climate change while supporting their communities, improving diversity and inclusion, and building more ethical business practices.

Public Sector and Private Institution Partnerships Lead to a Brighter Future

Social impact is not a spectator sport. There's something all of us can do to help solve some of the world's most pressing issues.
Tiger Tyagarajan, chief executive officer, Genpact

Addressing difficult challenges requires that people and organizations work together, sharing their knowledge and expertise. As Tiger Tyagarajan says, social impact is not a spectator sport. There's something all of us can do to help solve some of the world's most pressing issues. Increasingly that means that companies must take the lead, as progress on the government side comes in fits and starts. For example, in the climate arena, getting governments to agree on urgent measures has been difficult.

Public–private partnerships are emphasizing a few important priorities, including:

- **Getting started.** Difficult challenges can be intimidating. But taking the first step is imperative. Even incremental action is better than no action.
- **Removing barriers.** Providing access to opportunity, education, and healthcare requires that governments, the private sector, and private citizens work together. We must show up for each other and assist those in historically undeveloped and underserved communities.
- **Creating ecosystems of impact.** When we bring groups together to tackle incredibly complex problems, diversity of thought and expertise in perspectives, all catalyzed around a common goal, amplify our potential.
- **Building skills.** Leveraging expertise and talent will enable companies to tackle climate change and other pressing issues. That's why it's so important to reskill and upskill employees to complement the rise of automation. It will not only enhance operations but also increase the adoption and integration of digital technologies and AI.

As an example, Climate Vault and Genpact are collaborating to address and solve climate change. By applying advanced digital technologies to Climate Vault's world's first quantifiable, verifiable, transparent, and integrated carbon reduction and removal solution, they are supercharging the ability for organizations and people to have a bigger, faster impact on climate change. This is accomplished by enhancing the transparency, accuracy, and effectiveness of their carbon reduction and removal efforts.

By using digital technologies such as blockchain and machine learning, Climate Vault is able to provide a more accurate and verifiable measurement of carbon offsets and removals. This helps to increase transparency and accountability, as organizations and individuals can be confident that their efforts are making a real and measurable impact on reducing carbon emissions.

In addition, Climate Vault's use of advanced digital technologies allows for more efficient and effective management of carbon offsets and removals. By automating certain processes and utilizing data analytics, Climate Vault is able to identify and prioritize the most impactful projects and strategies for reducing carbon emissions. This can lead to a faster and more effective response to climate change, as organizations and individuals are able to focus their efforts on the most impactful areas.

How AI Will Change Creativity and Human Experiences

By now, we are used to the idea that AI is becoming incredibly powerful. It can create artwork and essays and write code. It will become even more capable in the future.

That's good news—for both businesses and employees. This revolutionary technology will enable people to address old problems in new ways. For example, predictive intelligence can forecast the impact of various choices, so users can be intentional about the decisions they make.

Predictive intelligence uses machine learning algorithms and statistical models to analyze past data and make predictions about future outcomes. By leveraging data and analytics, predictive intelligence can help users make informed decisions and forecast the impact of various choices.

Examples of this are

- **Analyzing past data:** Predictive intelligence can analyze past data to identify patterns and trends. This can help users understand how different decisions have impacted similar situations in the past, and make more informed choices based on this information.
- **Identifying potential outcomes:** Predictive intelligence can use data to identify potential outcomes for different choices. For example, it can forecast the potential impact of different marketing strategies, or the likelihood of success for a particular investment.
- **Recommending optimal choices:** Based on the analysis of past data and the identification of potential outcomes, predictive intelligence can recommend the optimal choice for a given situation. This can help users make informed decisions and achieve better outcomes.
- **Providing real-time insights:** Predictive intelligence can provide real-time insights into the impact of different choices, allowing users to adjust their decisions and strategies accordingly.

Providing these types of data-driven insights and recommendations can lead to better and more successful outcomes over time.

Bringing data-led insights together with the people who understand business, industry, and processes will allow them to apply their—very human—skills and judgment. This is how data helps people make the best decisions—for the organization, its employees, and the communities it operates in.

Look at it this way: critical data is often hidden in unstructured documents, flat files, and even manual reports. AI speeds up data ingestion, extraction, and classification. At the same time, it helps change behavior—providing thoughtful and timely nudges, many of which we have perfected with digital commerce, such as how Nike utilizes a smart notification system that informs the user about the popularity of a product by displaying the total number of units sold. Also, the notification encourages the user to join other trendsetters in purchasing the product while it remains popular. Where machine intelligence is concerned, a human-in-the-loop approach produces the best results.

A second important benefit of adopting AI in the workplace is that it will enhance the employee experience. AI will liberate people to focus on higher-value tasks and responsibilities, making jobs more interesting, fun, and rewarding.

Which human quality will best serve employees in this fast-changing world of AI? Curiosity, without question. The curious person, one who thirsts for new experiences, knowledge, and ideas, will propel the organization into the future.

4

Digital Transformation Models and Digital Disruption

As we enter a new era of technology-driven customer service, businesses must adapt their operations to meet the demands of the digital age. Digital transformation is forcing companies to reevaluate their business models and find ways to better serve customers anytime, anywhere, in the format and on the device of their choosing. To do this, businesses must proactively invest in technology and take advantage of the opportunities presented by cutting-edge solutions. This chapter highlights some of the models that have emerged as a result of AI and the disruption caused by the digital revolution and its overall impact on society as a whole.

New Models Evolving

Progress has shown that companies that fail to invest in digital transformation risk falling behind their competitors and, eventually, suffering from lost market share and financial losses. On the other hand, those that embrace digital transformation can bring greater value to customers through a more relevant customer experience.

In fact, research demonstrates that highly engaged customers are more likely to purchase frequently, spend more per purchase, and have three times the annual value compared to the average customer. Other statistics reveal that 35% of executives credit digital transformation with helping them reach customer expectations and improve operational efficiency, and 38% of executives plan to invest even more in technology to make it their competitive advantage.

For example, the concept of the "always connected customer" has opened up new opportunities in subscription-based models, as customers are now more likely to subscribe to services or products they use on a regular basis. Moreover, companies are beginning to focus on customer lifetime value rather than on one-time purchases, creating a more sustainable and profitable business model.

The takeaway is clear: to remain competitive, businesses must be willing to embrace digital transformation and evolve their models to meet customer expectations. By actively investing in technology solutions and focusing on customer engagement, companies can create an unmatched experience for their customers and ultimately drive long-term success. This is where the conversation regarding perception of value comes in.

Changing Perception of Value

Think about the way people have changed their attitudes and expectations toward businesses in the digital age. The proliferation of technology has shifted the way companies do business, and customer expectations have risen with that shift. Customers now expect to be able to purchase goods or services at any time, from anywhere, on any device. They want a personalized experience that reflects their individual needs and preferences. They demand convenience and expect quick response times, even when dealing with highly complex problems.

In addition, customers now have a heightened awareness of corporate social responsibility. Social responsibility is no longer just an option; it has become a key driver in customer decision-making. Companies that demonstrate commitment to sustainability, ethical practices, and other initiatives that prioritize the well-being of their customers and the environment are increasingly viewed as more valuable than companies that don't. As a result, candidates have been shown to accept substantially lower pay offers when those offers come from companies with a strong brand and focus on sustainability.

Car manufacturers are a prime example of an industry that is shifting its focus to meet the changing needs of customers. In the past, car manufacturers emphasized features such as top speed and acceleration, which appealed to drivers. Now, with self-driving cars on the horizon and the popularity of ride-sharing services, consumer perceptions of what's important have changed. Riders now value amenities more than drivers, and car manufacturers must make sure they are adapting their models to meet these changing expectations.

Therefore, we see that digital transformation has a profound effect not only on individual industries but on value perception as a whole. Efficiency, convenience, and ease of use are now the currency in this new digital economy, and companies must make sure they have the technology solutions in place to keep up with customer expectations.

Immediate Customer Feedback

Instantaneous. That's the new expectation for customer service, and it's no surprise why: technology has confirmed that customers are more informed than ever before. With a near-constant appetite to consume content online, customers now expect companies to provide immediate response times and personalized experiences.

Today's customers want an ongoing relationship with their preferred brands and companies. They want to be able to access customer support any time, from anywhere. And they expect that customer experience to be tailored to their individual needs and preferences. In a digitally transformed world, it's essential for businesses to provide immediate feedback and response times in order to meet customer expectations.

According to a study by Hubspot, 90% of customers rate immediate responses to their questions and concerns as important or very important.[1] Another study by Motista reveals that customers with an emotional connection to a brand have three times the lifetime value of those who don't, and are 30% more likely to recommend the brand to others.[2]

The implications of these findings are clear: customers today demand more than just a transaction. They want a relationship with the brands and companies they choose to engage with, and that requires businesses to provide an excellent customer experience through immediate feedback and response times. The imperative for companies is to invest in technologies and solutions that provide this level of service in order to remain competitive.

Impact on Community and Society

The digitization of our world has both undoubted benefits as well as pressing issues that need to be addressed. The use of AI and big data in the health sector, for example, has allowed medical professionals to diagnose diseases more accurately and save lives. Virtual learning environments have also increased access to education for those who may otherwise have been excluded. Blockchain technology has made public services more accessible and accountable.

However, although those who have access to these technologies are able to reap the benefits, there is a growing digital divide that risks leaving many behind. Women, the elderly, and ethnic and linguistic minorities may lack the necessary resources to access this technology effectively. Worryingly, the pace of connectivity among these groups is slowing, or even reversing.

In order to ensure that everyone has access to the benefits of digital technology, governments and businesses must take measures to bridge this gap. This includes investing in infrastructure, providing training opportunities, and offering financial assistance for those who are unable to cover the costs associated with accessing digital technologies. Additionally, ethical considerations must be taken into account—the use of such technologies should not be used to further marginalize or disadvantage certain groups.

We are experiencing a third wave of digitization, one with the potential to have a dramatic impact on many aspects of our lives. As with the first and second waves, this third wave offers significant social and economic opportunities but also carries risks. Research from McKinsey suggests that 45% of tasks undertaken by US workers are automatable with existing technology, while in Europe, 45% of jobs are at risk of automation.[3]

The third wave is likely to result in an increase in business efficiencies, but also job destruction for low-skilled workers. Furthermore, the number of people who are socioeconomically disadvantaged and disconnected from digital technologies is a major concern that cannot be ignored.

Therefore, it is necessary to ensure that policies and strategies are in place to support those at risk of being left behind.

The potential for this third wave of digitization should not be underestimated. Applications related to health, e-government services, and environmental sustainability can have a positive impact on the population. At the same time, e-government applications can reduce travel times needed to conduct transactions in public administrations.

With the UN's Sustainable Development Goals (SDGs) in mind, it is important that policymakers consider the potential of digital technologies and automation to create a fairer and more inclusive world. This includes making sure that those at risk of being left behind are adequately supported and provided with the tools they need to make use of the opportunities offered by this new wave of digitization. Education, training, and access to digital technologies will be key in ensuring that everyone can benefit from the potential of this third wave.

The evidence so far suggests that the third wave of digitization has been largely positive, but much uncertainty still surrounds its disruptive effects. Therefore, it is important to remain vigilant and take steps to mitigate any negative impacts that may arise. With the right policies in place, this third wave of digitization can help create a fairer and more sustainable future for all.

Culture of Collaboration

A culture of collaboration is a key component of a successful digital transformation strategy. It involves breaking down traditional silos and encouraging openness and collaboration between different stakeholders, such as governments, businesses, academia, and citizens. This can be achieved through fostering an open culture in which information is shared freely and ideas are encouraged to be developed collectively.

This kind of collaboration enables digital transformation to be supported by a wider range of perspectives and can help to ensure that it is both inclusive and beneficial for all stakeholders. The potential for an ecosystem of innovation is immense, with digital technologies being used to create innovative solutions to global challenges such as climate change and poverty.

To facilitate this kind of collaboration, there needs to be a commitment from all stakeholders to embrace the digital transformation and work together for a common goal. This commitment needs to be supported by the development of policies, strategies, and frameworks that ensure the effective use of digital technologies and automation. Moreover, it is important to ensure an equitable distribution of resources between different stakeholders, so that everyone can benefit from digital transformation.

Shifts Brought On by the Pandemic

The pandemic has caused a wave of disruption that has forced many businesses to reevaluate their existing practices and develop new ways of working. Many organizations have adopted agile approaches such as flatter, nonhierarchical structures, project-based working, and hub-and-spoke models with remote teams.

Each of these changes requires a shift in the traditional mindset and culture, as well as an attitude of collaboration among all stakeholders. This is because effective digital transformation requires organizations to be open to trying new approaches and processes that can result in innovative solutions. However, this kind of collaborative approach also needs to be supported by adequate resources and infrastructure.

For example, remote working requires reliable Internet access, secure digital platforms and tools, and comprehensive training programs. Moreover, organizations need to ensure that there is an equitable allocation of resources among all stakeholders in order to create an equal opportunity for everyone to participate in the digital transformation process.

The pandemic has provided a unique opportunity for business leaders to rethink their organizational strategies and develop new approaches to innovation. Investing in digital technologies and infrastructure is not only beneficial for the organization, it also opens up possibilities for collaboration among different stakeholders. This kind of collaborative approach can help to ensure that digital transformation efforts are both inclusive and effective.

Digital transformation simultaneously requires businesses to adapt and enables them to do so. By embracing digital transformation, an enterprise can keep up with an evolving market and consumer expectations while addressing challenges to a disruption such as a pandemic.

In order to effectively implement digital transformation, organizations must focus on creating a technology platform that is flexible and adaptable. This means transitioning from legacy systems to "componentized" digital technologies—or building blocks—that are designed to be more easily reassembled and rearchitected. By leveraging such components, businesses can quickly adjust to changing needs and stay ahead of the competition.

For instance, a componentized system can provide a higher degree of agility and scalability, which is essential for companies that need to adjust their offerings in response to customer preferences. Additionally, this kind of technology platform enables businesses to leverage data from multiple sources, allowing them to gain deeper insights into customers' needs and wants.

Furthermore, such systems are also built with an eye toward the future. By taking advantage of componentized technology, companies can stay at the forefront of developing trends and even anticipate them before they take hold. This allows businesses to remain competitive in their respective markets and keep up with technological advances and consumer demands.

Examples of Digital Disruption

The impact of disruptive technologies and business models has been felt across industries, through their ability to both spark new innovations and disrupt existing ones. While the implications of these disruptions are far-reaching and often unpredictable, one thing is certain: in order for companies to remain competitive in this ever-changing landscape, they must be able to quickly and efficiently adapt to these new realities.

In the automotive industry, for example, we have seen a shift in consumer preferences toward car-sharing services such as Zipcar and Uber, leading to an increase in demand for connected vehicles. This trend has led to the development of advanced safety features and autonomous driving capabilities as automakers strive to meet customer demands while maintaining their competitive edge.

Meanwhile, the emergence of streaming services like Netflix and Hulu have revolutionized the way people consume media content, disrupting traditional cable companies in the process. This shift has led to an increase in demand for tailored viewing experiences and personalization options, leading to innovations such as on-demand streaming, personalized recommendations, and interactive content.

Finally, the rise of collaborative commerce has enabled an unprecedented level of fluidity in the marketplace. Companies such as Airbnb and

Uber have disrupted traditional business models by creating new ways of understanding value exchange among buyers and sellers across a wide range of industries. As more companies continue to embrace this model, we can expect to see further progress in terms of enhanced customer service, transparency, and efficiency throughout the business landscape.

Overall, it is clear that disruptive technologies and business models are here to stay, and companies must be prepared to both anticipate and respond to them in order to remain competitive. By understanding the potential implications of these disruptions and actively adapting their business strategies accordingly, organizations will be better positioned to take advantage of the opportunities presented by these innovations. In doing so, they can also remain at the forefront of their respective industries and continue to drive innovation in new and exciting ways.

Expert Analysis: AI: The Most Digital Disruptive Transformation Model That Will Benefit Humankind

By Sylvain Duranton, Global Leader, BCG X, and Senior Partner and Managing Director, Boston Consulting Group

AI is an integral part of almost every aspect of our daily lives and is being integrated with other technologies. It is ubiquitous and will continue to be at the forefront of the next generation of technology. AI is the most essential and disruptive technology of the day with the potential to benefit mankind.

How can a company balance the rate of innovation, financial performance, and business transformation?

While everyone agrees that their AI strategy must be linked with their business strategy, they tend to spread their resources thinly across all topics and not take strong strategic bets and direction. A company needs to make choices and strong allocations, which is the essence of strategy. By linking AI strategy with business strategy, a company can achieve massive improvements in business performance, but this requires reorganizing fully the function and people who make decisions, building AI at scale engines, and pushing.

Two examples of disruptive technologies that improved business performance are as follows:

- Using AI to steer pricing and promotion helped a large mass retailer to create value of one to three additional points of margin.
- Helping individual farmers in Southeast Asia improve their farming practice by giving specific tips through iPhones based on weather and soil conditions and diseases enabled them to increase their crop yields.

As business leaders, it's important to consistently keep humans in the AI loop, regardless of the strategy being used, such as creativity or marketing. Let's take the example of a generative AI portal. I believe it will have a significant impact on productivity for many people. You can use general AI models, such as those from Microsoft, to boost the productivity of programmers, but it doesn't replace them entirely. Instead, it can accelerate testing, which is a tedious part of programming that can't be fully automated using large models. Documentation is also a tedious task that many programmers and developers don't enjoy, but large models can provide significant help in scaling the process.

To accelerate research in this field, we encoded years of research literature and used ML [machine learning] and generative AI to identify potential matches for effective mechanisms of action. However, we are not trying to replace researchers, as breakthrough experiments and article writing still require human involvement. Our goal is to help guide people and accelerate the process of launching experiments by suggesting potential matches. The ultimate decision on which bet to take is still up to humans, and they will be the ones conducting the tests based on the initial research and knowledge. By using AI to suggest matches, we save time and increase the likelihood of success.

Generative AI can be very useful for quickly sketching concepts and providing ideas to designers, but ultimately a designer is still

(continued)

needed to fully interpret the output. It's important to remain humble and recognize that GPT is not infallible and requires human oversight.

AI can be helpful in fields such as cancer cohorts, where it can be used to predict outcomes and guide treatment decisions, but it's still important for doctors to make decisions and recommendations based on their own expertise. While automation can be useful in fields such as surgery, it's unlikely that complete automation without human oversight will be feasible in the foreseeable future. Many successful companies have codified their own way of managing the interface between AI technology and human involvement, recognizing the importance of a human-centric approach. In fields such as trucking, even with increasing automation, experts will still be needed for quality assurance and monitoring.

Digital Resiliency

As the digital transformation of business continues to march forward, companies must ensure that they are well-positioned for the future. Chief among their responsibilities is developing a culture of digital resiliency: the ability to anticipate and quickly adapt to changes in the dynamic world of digital technology. This can be achieved through fostering an agile culture, innovative use of data, and leveraging the power of artificial intelligence (AI) to gain a competitive advantage.

Digital agility is essential in order to ensure that business processes are resilient enough to address issues quickly and effectively when they arise. Companies must be able to react promptly to changing consumer needs and technological advances. Through an agile approach, businesses can get ahead of the competition by being prepared for market shifts and having the ability to anticipate customer needs.

Data is one of the most valuable assets a company can possess. It allows companies to uncover insights that inform decision-making, help define their competitive advantages, and better understand customer behaviors. By leveraging data analysis technology, companies can gain an advantage over the competition, as well as uncover new opportunities for growth.

AI also provides invaluable insights into customer behavior and preferences, which can be leveraged to develop smarter marketing strategies and personalized products. H&M Group has been at the forefront of leveraging AI-driven technology to deliver innovative solutions that drive revenue and better serve customers. Examples include predictive analytics to forecast market demand, automated warehouses that offer next-day deliveries, personalized in-store experiences driven by RFID technology, and tailor-made clothing.

In addition to H&M, Levi Strauss & Co. is another example of a company that is leading the way in leveraging AI-driven technology to gain an edge. The company has been using AI-assisted design technology to expedite the creative process. The company's algorithm is capable of defining edges, locating button placements, and determining pockets for garments. With a single click, it can generate thousands of design options that then have to be narrowed down through human influence. This allows for fast production and ensures that each garment design is of a high quality.

The public sector is at the forefront of adapting to digital transformation, with initiatives such as Singapore's SkillsFuture program. This program seeks to equip students with the skills needed for a successful career in the digital age by providing subsidies for courses relating to areas like engineering and blockchain system planning. The Ministry of Education is also partnering with other government agencies and private businesses to ensure that the workforce is adequately prepared for the digital age.

Estonia has embraced digital transformation and established itself as an example of digital resilience. By recognizing Internet access as a basic human right, the country has achieved nearly universal online access among its 1.3 million residents. This commitment to digital inclusion demonstrates Estonia's dedication to establishing a citizen-centric form of governance.

The Estonian government has used digital transformation to create a "zero bureaucracy" experience by streamlining and partially automating public services. AI is being used in various sectors, like unemployment insurance, customer support calls, and road accident predictions to improve service delivery. Predictive analytics are also being used to ensure farmers comply with subsidy regulations and detect flooding risks for better building plan decisions. These initiatives have enabled the government to anticipate and respond to citizens' needs, thereby increasing efficiency and reducing costs.

Estonia's commitment to digital transformation is also evident in its plans for a consent management platform that will enable citizens to manage how their information is accessed and shared. With this initiative, Estonia has positioned itself as an example of digital resilience and is setting the standard for public service delivery. By continuing to invest in emerging technologies, Estonia is demonstrating its commitment to a more equitable and secure digital future.

The Kingdom of Saudi Arabia has demonstrated its commitment to digital resilience by investing heavily in smart city initiatives. With plans to build 200 smart cities across the country, the government is embracing emerging technologies such as AI to improve citizens' quality of life and stimulate economic growth. For example, AI is being used to design better urban landscapes and encourage smart solutions in the Kingdom.

This commitment is also evident in their plans to establish a consent management platform, allowing citizens to manage how their information is accessed and shared. These initiatives ensure that Saudi Arabia remains at the forefront of digital technology and is better equipped to handle any potential disruptions in the future.

The Kingdom's investment in smart cities has resulted in a significant market growth, with the Saudi Arabia smart cities' market size being valued at $3,552.1 million in 2019, and projected to reach $14,745.2 million by 2027—a compound annual growth rate of 19.6% from 2020 to 2027.[4] These remarkable achievements display the country's strong commitment toward digital resilience and set an example for other nations to follow. As such, Saudi Arabia is paving the way for a more secure and equitable digital future. The Kingdom is setting a benchmark for digital resilience that will allow citizens around the world to benefit from technological advances and ensure a safe, prosperous future.

BlackRock's Global Impact Fund is committed to providing investors with the tools they need to build resilient portfolios that are aligned with the UN's SDGs. By actively investing in global companies whose products and services address pressing social and environmental issues, the fund provides access to differentiated sources of alpha while generating an impact on people and the planet.

The fund is not only focused on achieving financial returns, but also on helping mitigate risk and ensuring portfolio resilience in the face of digital disruptions. To this end, it applies best practices related to digital resilience across all aspects of its operations—from managing data security to developing innovative products and services such as blockchain-based solutions. For instance, the fund is leveraging AI to identify investment opportunities that can help increase the resilience of portfolios while offering superior returns.

In addition, BlackRock is actively engaging with regulators and policymakers in order to ensure that digital investments comply with applicable laws and regulations. The company also works closely with clients to provide them with robust digital solutions that help them manage risk and ensure portfolio resilience in the face of digital disruptions. These efforts demonstrate BlackRock's commitment to building a more resilient, equitable, and sustainable future for all.

By investing in global impact funds with a focus on digital resilience, investors can not only benefit from superior returns but also help drive much-needed changes and build a more equitable world.

Expert Input and Analysis: As We Embrace AI, We Must Ensure We Fully Understand the Ethical Questions It Poses

By Atti Riazi, Senior Vice President and Chief Information Officer, Hearst Corporation

Hearst's sustainability efforts align with strategic pillars: educating the public, lowering Hearst's carbon emissions, and investing in B2B solutions that enable other corporations to achieve their climate goals.

Responsible environmental stewardship has long been an integral part of the way Hearst does business. We recognized that Hearst needed to showcase the many initiatives in one place in order to educate employees, business partners, advertisers, and even potential talent about the broad efforts already underway. David Carey, Senior VP, Public Affairs and Communications of Hearst, believes that "although we're not a public company and aren't required to report on our greenhouse gas emissions, we feel that it is the right thing to do. We conducted a holistic analysis of Hearst's carbon footprint with the help of climate experts and complemented that with a snapshot

(continued)

of our initiatives to educate the public and invest inB2B solutions that further positive environmental change."

Creating B2B solutions to help other corporations meet their climate/sustainability goals

We have several venture investing teams looking for the companies and founders who are innovating and shaping the world. Quite organically, there's been a great deal of new product development specifically geared toward sustainability. The opportunity to enable other corporations and even startups to further their ability to collect, analyze, and create action plans based on environmental data is consistent with Hearst's overarching commitment to operating in an environmentally responsible manner.

Solutions Hearst has had a hand in creating

Hearst Transportation companies proactively embrace the rapid advancement of electric vehicle technologies. A recent acquisition, Noregon Systems, provides advanced commercial vehicle diagnostic repair and monitoring applications that help maximize vehicle uptime. The company includes the latest EV repair diagnostic procedure information for commercial vehicles in each new release of its flagship diagnostic software. Accounting for air travel, CAMP Systems International has been part of the Hearst portfolio since 2016 and works to lower the environmental impact of business jets and helicopters globally by reducing fuel consumption and emissions through optimized engine performance.

Dropcountr, another application-based Hearst investment, is a cloud-based water analytics platform that translates water meter data into actionable information for utility customers and staff, who can now monitor their water use and optimize conservation. And cloud-based monitoring means a lot less paper reporting for the municipalities and other customers who rely on Dropcountr data.

An exciting future positively impacting society and the planet

Hearst is only at the beginning of its sustainability journey, and it is exciting to be at the intersection of such potential and scalability that comes with our incredibly diverse business operations and forward-thinking leadership. Through recent investments in trailblazing, data-driven companies and best-in-class talent, Hearst has made it clear that environmentally responsible technology solutions are the way forward. The robust framework offered by the three-pronged sustainability strategy—educating the public about climate issues, reducing our own carbon footprint, and investing in solutions that help others reach climate goals—will continue to guide our business operations as we work toward a multi-year progression of data collection and emission reduction.

As we embrace AI, we must ensure that we fully understand the ethical questions it poses and advocate for a full dialogue around its implications both short and long term, positive and negative. Innovation brings great transformation and without innovation we are all doomed to stagnation and entropy. However, responsible innovation, where we fully understand its impact on society, human life, climate, economy, politics, and culture, is essential. Advancements in technology, especially within the AI space, will bring broad innovations in healthcare, education, food, supply chain, climate, closing the digital divide, and helping address some of the critical and deep social issues. Let's ensure that we embrace innovation consciously and responsibly.

The Issue of Privacy

With enterprises, businesses, and governmental agencies using so much of our information, how do we protect that information from malicious actors?

Back in 2018, the world woke up to two cases that sent shockwaves across the data privacy space. The first one was Cambridge Analytica's unethical use of users' data collected through Facebook's API loophole and targeting them with ad campaigns for the 2016 US presidential election.

This incident showed how vulnerable user data can be if it is not properly secured and monitored.

The second incident was the implementation of a Social Credit System in China, wherein people's trustworthiness and behavior is rated based on surveillance data collected through 200 million cameras and facial recognition. This AI-based system has resulted in an unprecedented political stranglehold by the Chinese government over its citizens, further raising questions about data privacy.

These two cases make it crystal clear that data privacy is becoming even more vulnerable as AI is being used to collect and analyze large amounts of personal data. AI algorithms are now being used for surveillance, facial recognition, and analyzing user behavior, which raises a number of ethical questions about how AI should be used in the context of data privacy.

AI for good is an emerging concept of using technology to improve people's lives and solve pressing problems. As the world moves toward an increasingly digital age, AI has become an important tool for fraud prevention and financial management, especially in the context of government agencies who have access to large sums of money.

The federal budget is too vast for traditional tools like manual auditing to keep track of, and many government systems are antiquated and unable to handle the rapid growth in data analytics. To address this issue, AI algorithms are being used for fraud detection, budget oversight, personnel performance tracking, and organizational activities.

AI-based solutions have already been deployed by private sector organizations such as banks and hospitals to monitor financial transactions and ensure that their customers are following proper procedures. These solutions have proven to be effective in detecting fraud and reducing the amount of time and money spent on manual auditing.

For example, banks have reported investing over $217 billion in 2021 to implement AI applications for fraud prevention, with 64% of financial institutions believing AI can anticipate and prevent fraud before it happens.[5]

Insurance companies have also been quick to deploy AI solutions for fraud prevention, with 44% of the largest insurers using AI to detect fraud, waste, and abuse in 2021. These AI solutions are designed to identify errors or unusual activity that could point to fraudulent activity. Software providers are offering a range of products designed to identify suspicious activity and errors that may indicate fraud. To start their own AI-based fraud detection processes, government agencies must ensure they have the necessary infrastructure and resources to support such software. They must also ensure that their algorithms are properly trained and monitored for accuracy, as AI-based solutions can only be successful when reliable sources of information are available.

The bottom line is that privacy is a key consideration when deploying AI solutions, and government agencies must take steps to ensure that any data collected is securely stored and managed.

The Role of AI in Medicine, Human Capacity, and Humanitarian Missions

We have only scratched the surface of potential applications for AI in healthcare. AI systems can help NGOs reach more people with services and information they need—such as education, legal, and health information—freeing up human resources to focus on high-priority work. Additionally, AI can be used to make decisions and act faster in emergencies through real-time awareness of the situation, predict emergencies before they spread and escalate through early detection and warning, as well as improve outcomes through real-time feedback on the effectiveness of programs.

For example, the Danish Refugee Council is using AI/ML to forecast forced displacement in places like Burkina Faso, Mali, Niger, and Nigeria in West Africa. The International Rescue Committee is using AI/ML in a number of projects, including for optimizing service delivery to refugees, for predictive modeling of conflicts and crises, and to facilitate jobs-matching for refugees. The Norwegian Refugee Council's chatbot assists Venezuelan migrants in Colombia with learning their rights according to current immigration policies and laws. Lastly, the Carter Center is using AI to get more accurate and timely analysis on the Syrian conflict.

What we can take away from these examples is that AI can help NGOs gain valuable insights, reduce the risks of human errors, and allow researchers to focus on more complex cases. The technology is set to revolutionize the humanitarian sector over the coming years, helping NGOs make more informed decisions quickly and accurately while also freeing up resources to focus on high-priority areas. As such, it's essential for NGOs to begin experimenting with AI and ML technologies now, in order to make sure they stay ahead of the curve and continue to provide high-quality services to those who need it.

How Does AI Reshape Hospitals and Nursing Practices, and How Do People's Relationships Reshape Technology?

Imagine a world in which nurses can monitor their patients from miles away with AI-driven technologies and voice assistants. As we continue to face public health crises such as the COVID-19 pandemic, this reality is becoming more attainable. AI and ML solutions are helping to revolutionize healthcare and nursing practices by providing efficient ways of retrieving meaningful data from patients remotely and between clinic visits.

AI-driven software and chat boxes enable patients to communicate with automated systems, providing them with the information they need without having to contact the reception desk. Automation tools are also helping to relieve clinicians of mundane tasks and speed up processes, allowing them to focus on high-priority areas. Additionally, platforms such as mHealth and sensor-based technologies are being employed to monitor patient data from the comfort of their homes, which is particularly useful for managing chronic illnesses.

Voice assistants such as Amazon Alexa and Google Assistant have become popular tools in electronic health record (EHR) applications. For example, they can be used to remind patients to take medications or measure blood pressure, then record this data in the EHR for a nurse to review.

Ultimately, AI will continue to play an increasingly important role in healthcare and nursing practices as we strive toward improved treatment outcomes for all. With the right technologies in place, clinicians can provide the best care to their patients and be one step closer to achieving our greatest health ambitions. By leveraging these types of technologies, nurses are able to better manage their patients' care, especially when resources and staffing are limited.

Create Your Organization's Vision of the Future

Every organization should adopt AI as an integral part of how it develops its strategy, serves its constituents, and operates daily.

As a first step, organizations need to create the vision for their future— for example, asking themselves questions about the overarching opportunity

Expert Input and Analysis: Applications of Data and AI at Scale to Reimagine the Future with a Focus on Sustainability

By Katia Walsh, PhD, award-winning global technology, data, and AI cross-industry leader; Fortune 500 board director; pioneer of digital upskilling and responsible AI

We are living in the time of the mainstreaming of AI. AI is now part of how everybody lives their daily life, conducts business operations, and functions in society. This means that AI at scale is already becoming a part of various industries.

For example, in manufacturing, AI predicts and minimizes carbon emissions. In fulfillment, AI optimizes a number of factors, balancing delivery speed, costs and profit margin, number of shipments, and packaging all at once. AI can even save fashion—one of the industries that has, until recently, not been a good citizen of our planet. With AI, apparel companies no longer need to make trade-offs between profitability and sustainability, or profitability and creativity. Through machine learning algorithms, they can achieve creativity, profitability, and sustainability all at once and keep improving continuously to be the responsible citizens of our planet we need in every industry.

The greatest potential for AI's positive impact

It's hard and probably unfair to single out a specific AI application. AI has already revolutionized the nature of business. Remember the four Ps of marketing: product, price, place, and promotion? Now, thanks to AI, there are new four Ps in defining a modern business: predictive, proactive, personalized, and precise. AI applications improve the customer experience, deliver internal efficiencies, create new business models, and contribute to social good and sustainability.

In the areas of what I consider universal rights—healthcare, education, and employment opportunities—AI can be especially impactful. The technology helps deliver prevention, develop medications, and target their effect in individualized treatments, to name a few

(continued)

applications in healthcare alone. In education, AI has the potential to enable global-scale teaching and research platforms that power life-long learning. And in the workplace, AI—developed by diverse people, using diverse data, and sharing diverse tools—will minimize bias, unearth candidates who may not have been identified by traditional methods, and chart unique new career paths.

Criteria to assess the social impact of technology

There are several criteria that can help us assess—and goals to set for—the impact of technology. First is the Hippocratic oath equivalent of "do no harm." After that, we can judge the impact of technology by its ability to:

- Create fairness and empowerment of all people, regardless of socio-economic status;
- Connect, rather than isolate;
- Predict with accuracy and shine a light in uncertain times;
- Enable and nudge people to act on those predictions and prevent negative events whenever possible.

There can be many objectives and key results for AI to shine with its social impact. These are just a few examples at this time. The list will expand as this field continuously advances.

How can institutions work together to govern AI in a way that benefits society?

Technology (even AI) in and of itself is neutral. It's the people and organizations who develop and apply the technology that determine whether it can benefit or harm society. Institutions around the world have a responsibility to ensure they do all they can to encourage beneficial applications, prevent unintended consequences, or punish potentially harmful targeting of the technology. Examples include, but are not limited, to:

- Sharing data (anonymized and aggregated) freely and openly for common use toward universal social good;
- Mobilizing researchers around the world to band together with joint research, publications, and applications in a collaborative spirit;
- Creating and distributing shared ethics principles;
- Developing and implementing best practices for using AI in responsible ways;
- Updating regulations to continuously keep up with technology advances;
- Holding accountable the organizations and people who create, use, and scale AI and setting the highest standards, instead of settling for the lowest common denominator;
- Conducting open "post-mortem" discussions to share lessons learned and encourage responsible experimentation;
- Enforcing accountability measures to curb bad actors swiftly and consistently;
- Continuously educating leaders, communities, organizations, business, and society on the need for responsible AI applications and not compromising on standing up for what's right—the world and the technology deserve nothing less.

they seek to seize or the high-value problem they can help solve for business or society.

As a next step, organizations need to plan the development of an AI capability, then mobilize the people, processes, data, and infrastructure for AI applications. Crucially, they need to immediately start delivering measurable value from AI applications—particularly in an area of the organization that is meaningful and will serve as a champion of the new capability. Over time, AI applications will expand to more problems to solve, more markets to serve, and more functions to power—until AI begins to penetrate the entirety of a business or government organization.

This is already happening: AI today is where mobile was a decade ago. In a decade (or less), AI will be all around us and ubiquitous in use.

People and countries that may be behind in tech today will leapfrog and surpass some that may seem ahead today. The question is not what the future of AI is. The question is: What comes after AI and how do we harness it for good?

Expert Input and Analysis: Reimagining the Future of the Industry with a Focus on Sustainability
By Alan Boehme, Chief Technology Officer at H&M Group

The ability to take in and absorb a vast variety of information, commercial, regulatory, sustainability climate, and so on, and run a vast number of scenarios will give us the ability to get mankind to envision a more holistic view of the future.

I believe the greatest impact that AI will have on the future of humanity is its positive impact on mental health and well-being.

We can only get to this future if there is a true public and private partnership looking and assessing specific measurements related to expected benefits as well as the cost to provide them.

5 | Technologies Driving Society's Digital Transformation

This chapter discusses self-improving AI and explores the evolution of artificial intelligence and the concept of AI systems that are capable of self-improvement over time. It also delves into the use of artificial neural networks in AI, which is a technique inspired by the structure and function of the human brain.

In addition to discussing the advancements in AI technology, the chapter explores how these technologies can be used to empower cities and humanity as a whole. The application of AI in urban environments has the potential to improve transportation systems, enhance public safety, and streamline city services.

Looking toward the far future, the chapter also considers the potential implications of AI and neural network evolution on society and humanity as a whole. As these technologies continue to evolve and improve, it is important to consider the ethical and societal implications of their widespread adoption and use.

Deep Learning

The field of deep learning has come a long way since it first emerged in the 1980s. From the early days of limited computing power and data availability to today's state-of-the-art models, deep learning has revolutionized the way we approach problem solving across many industries.

A major breakthrough came in 2010 with the launch of the ImageNet competition, which made a large dataset of labeled images available to the public. This provided a platform to develop state-of-the-art image classifiers and kickstarted a convolutional neural network renaissance in the deep learning community. In 2011, AlexNet was developed and further accelerated progress in this field. In 2014, generative adversarial networks (GANs) emerged as the biggest breakthrough in modern deep learning at that time.

Today, deep learning is ubiquitous and used in a variety of applications. It has been used to determine which online ads to display in real time, identify and tag friends in photos, translate voice to text, translate text into different languages on a web page, and drive autonomous vehicles. Deep learning is also being used in less visible places such as credit card companies for fraud detection, businesses to predict personalization and customer cancellation risk, banks to predict bankruptcy and loan default risk, and hospitals to detect diseases.

Looking forward, the possibilities of deep learning are almost limitless. We are already seeing the development of new neural network architectures such as GANs (capable of generating art and music like humans), Siamese networks (classification of images through one-shot learning), and OpenAI's GPT-2 model (capable of generating coherent paragraphs of texts, reading comprehension, and text summarization with human-level accuracy). We are getting closer and closer to building deep learning–based systems that can adequately mimic the complex functionalities of a mature human brain.

In the near future, we can look forward to deep learning systems that far surpass human intelligence, resulting in advanced cognitive systems that can intelligently and fluently interact with humans. We are living in an exciting time as we witness technology changing the way we interact with our environment and solve complex problems. Moreover, quantum and emerging AI technologies promise to further revolutionize society's digital transformation.

Quantum and Emerging AI Technologies

Picture a world in which technology has advanced to a point of intelligent fluency, enabling us to solve complex problems easily and efficiently. This is the future of AI, and it's becoming more and more of a reality every day.

Advances in deep learning are paving the way for AI systems that can achieve human-level accuracy in recognizing patterns and processing information. With the right data sets, deep learning can revolutionize almost any industry or sector, from healthcare to finance to education. We are already seeing this with AI-based applications such as personal assistants, chatbots, facial recognition systems, and other advanced cognitive technologies.

Quantum computing is a new frontier of computer science that takes advantage of the laws of quantum mechanics to process information and find patterns in data that are not possible with conventional computers. With this technology, AI algorithms can be made more effective by analyzing a wider range of data and coming to better conclusions than conventional computers can.

Businesses and organizations of all sizes are beginning to explore the potential applications of AI and quantum computing. For example, AI assistants can be used as tutors, travel agents, or tax preparers. In aviation, autopilots are being designed to learn how to adapt to changing conditions by studying pilot actions and sorting through flight data. AI is also being used in healthcare for diagnostics, precision treatments, and personalized medicine.

Smart IoT Products

The Internet of Things (IoT) is a rapidly growing technology that connects everyday objects to the Internet. Smart products such as refrigerators, watches, and home gyms collect data and share it with their parent companies through the IoT. This vast network of connected devices gives businesses an unprecedented amount of data on consumer behavior that can be used to improve the customer experience.

Collecting data from these connected devices is just the first step in digital transformation. Companies can use machine learning systems to integrate and analyze this data to better understand patterns of user behavior.

Not only does this enable companies to predict maintenance issues with their products but it also provides insight into how prototypes should be designed for future products.

By utilizing the power of the IoT, companies can work together with their customers to customize experiences and provide an even higher level of value. This collaboration not only benefits customers but also gives businesses a competitive edge in the market. Through digital transformation, businesses can gain a deeper understanding of user behavior and tailor their products and services accordingly.

Collaborative Platforms

The power of collaboration has been forever changed by the introduction of digital platforms such as Zoom, WhatsApp, and FaceTime. These tools enable people to easily connect with one another, regardless of their location or time zone. This means that businesses can now create teams comprised of individuals from all across the globe.

Think about how this has revolutionized the way businesses operate. Companies can now easily access new talent, increase collaboration within departments, and improve communication among teams. Additionally, these tools are also beneficial for local businesses that may be geographically dispersed; they can use these platforms to connect with their customers or suppliers in real time.

Collaborative digital platforms have had a profound effect on innovation in the enterprise, allowing companies to quickly brainstorm ideas and form meaningful connections with creative professionals. This increased level of collaboration has also enabled local businesses to move faster and stay ahead of their competition.

Wearable Devices

Wearable devices have become increasingly popular in recent years, and they are revolutionizing the way we interact with technology. Smartwatches and fitness trackers allow us to monitor our health and keep track of daily activities in real time.

These devices can also be utilized by businesses to enhance their operations. Wearable devices enable companies to track employee performance and monitor productivity in real time. This helps managers better understand how their employees are performing, allowing them to make more informed decisions when it comes to staffing and scheduling.

Smartphones have become a mainstay in many industries, including manufacturing. With these devices, companies can track productivity levels, sales figures, and supply chain performance in real time—ensuring that businesses are always running at optimal capacity. Thanks to this capability, businesses can be more adaptable and agile in their decision-making, ultimately giving them an advantage over competitors.

Digital Twins

Digital twins are revolutionizing the way businesses operate by providing a virtual replica of real-world devices and people. Data scientists can use these digital models to simulate real-world problems, allowing them to analyze performance or predict potential issues. This can be extremely helpful in a variety of industries, such as healthcare, transportation, and manufacturing.

For example, digital twins allow healthcare providers to analyze patient data more effectively by creating virtual simulations based on their medical records. This helps them better understand how a person's health is changing over time and make informed decisions about treatments or medications.

In the transportation industry, digital twins can help predict traffic patterns based on data collected from real-world conditions. This allows companies to optimize routes, create more efficient delivery services, and improve customer satisfaction.

Finally, in the manufacturing sector, digital twins can be used to simulate how products will perform under a variety of conditions and ensure that they meet industry standards. This helps companies identify potential issues before they become problems and helps them stay ahead of the competition.

Speech Recognition, Human Language Processing, and Computer Vision

Alexa and Siri are just the tip of the iceberg when it comes to automatic speech recognition (ASR). In the coming years, ASR technology is set to become more pervasive and useful as its capabilities expand. Already, ASR has found application in areas such as police body cams, where it can be used to record and transcribe important interactions. Moving forward, ASR is expected to feature truly multilingual models, rich standardized output objects, and be available to all at scale.

Furthermore, ASR is being envisioned as an AI with the capability of organic learning—able to understand and use new words and speech styles without outside guidance. Additionally, it will need to operate without bias in order to ensure ethical use of the technology.

The future of natural language processing (NLP) is also quite exciting, with machines that can interact with us on a human level and understand the deeper implications of our words and phrases. This would allow us to communicate more effectively with computers, creating opportunities for better predictions and insights—making them much more useful tools than they are today.

In tandem with this, computer vision is also on the rise, providing organizations with the capability to identify and classify objects in real time. This technology has already been implemented in areas such as facial recognition and pose estimation, but its potential applications are far-reaching. We can expect cloud computing services to help scale up deep learning solutions, as well as automated machine learning (AutoML) to reduce time-consuming tasks within the ML pipeline.

Overall, AI and ML are reaching a critical turning point in their evolution—moving from experimentation to implementation on a large scale.

What Is Next for Automatic Speech Recognition and Machine Translation?

As automated language technologies like ASR and neural machine translation (NMT) continue to develop, the potential for businesses to scale their operations and reach new markets is becoming more apparent. Not only are these techniques becoming more accurate and efficient as time progresses, but they are also reducing costs associated with localization.

Studies conducted by Lionbridge's R&D teams estimate that NMT is improving by 3–7% every year, as measured by editing distance. This an indication of how quickly these technologies are advancing and evolving. As demand for translation services continues to grow, fueled in part by the COVID-19 crisis, machine translation will be used more frequently for parts of the content with or without human translation supervision.

The adoption of NMT is opening up new opportunities for businesses to expand their reach and get products to markets faster at a lower cost. As consumers become accustomed to being able to access product information in their native language, it will become increasingly important for companies to meet this expectation in all their markets.

The cost and time reductions that NMT offers is being recognized across industries, from retail and finance to healthcare and education. Lastly, NMT also improves accuracy and consistency of translations, allowing companies to provide better customer service across multiple markets. As the technology continues to become more advanced, it will undoubtedly bring numerous advantages for businesses, including better quality and faster turnaround times.

Future of Self-Improving AI and Artificial Neural Networks

By Tsvi Gal, Head of Enterprise Technology Services (Infrastructure) at Memorial Sloan Kettering Cancer Center

The future of self-improving AI and artificial neural networks (I will use "AI" as a shorter way to reference both) is incredible. Self-improving AI systems are rapidly evolving and are getting smarter and more complex. The usage of such systems is explored and being applied in many applications. The systems are capable of analyzing large datasets and making decisions based on the data. Furthermore, using unsupervised machine learning, they can improve with little or no human intervention, allowing them to adapt and learn from their mistakes. As such, they can be used now in many industries, such as healthcare, finance, transportation, and robotics. As the technology continues to evolve, AI will continue to be used in more applications, and its capabilities will increase.

Some examples include:

■ **Autonomous vehicles:** AI can be used to power autonomous vehicles, allowing them to become increasingly accurate and efficient over time. Regardless of the current setbacks, we are going

(continued)

toward a world of self-driving trucks and trains, which will significantly improve the speed and accuracy of transportations (e.g.,
autonomous cars don't need to stop for breaks or sleep).

- **Smart homes:** AI can be used to make smart homes more efficient and responsive to the needs of their owners. The systems can
adjust the homes to the needs of the families as well as individuals
within the family and continue to learn their presences and needs.
- **Cybersecurity:** AI can be used to more effectively detect and
respond to cyber threats. It is especially good in detecting anomalies
and identifying "sleeper" malware.
- **Natural language processing:** AI can be used to create more
natural language processing systems, allowing for more accurate and
efficient communication between people and machines.
- **Smarter energy management:** AI can be used to optimize
energy usage, reduce waste and emissions, and promote a more sustainable future.
- **Improved education:** AI can be used to create personalized
learning experiences and to improve the quality of education in
schools, universities, and other educational institutions.
- **Improved agriculture:** AI can be used to optimize agricultural
processes and help farmers increase yields, reduce costs, and improve
the quality of their produce.

Specifically in healthcare, we should expect:

- **Identification and diagnosis of disease:** AI can be used to identify and diagnose diseases by analyzing large datasets of patient data
and medical records. This can help to speed up diagnosis and reduce
the amount of time spent on diagnosis.
- **Drug discovery:** AI can be used to analyze large datasets in order
to identify potential new drugs. This can help to reduce the amount
of time spent on drug discovery.
- **Personalized treatments:** AI can be used to analyze patient
data in order to provide personalized treatments tailored to each

individual patient. This can help to reduce the amount of time spent on treatments and improve outcomes.

- **Patient monitoring:** AI can be used to monitor patient data in order to detect any changes in the patient's condition. This can help to detect any signs of illness earlier and provide timely treatment.

Quantum

Quantum technology is still in its infancy, but its potential is great. The potential of quantum technology is immense and far-reaching. It promises to revolutionize the way computers process data, achieve unprecedented levels of security for communications, and enable extraordinary developments in areas such as artificial intelligence, drug development, and materials science. Quantum technology has the potential to revolutionize industries, from finance to healthcare, and its potential applications are only limited by our imagination. Quantum computing has the potential to revolutionize the way we process data and solve problems. Ultimately, the future of quantum technology depends on the commitment and investment of governments, companies, and research organizations to develop and commercialize these technologies.

Examples:

- **Quantum computing:** Quantum computing is being used to create more efficient and powerful algorithms for solving complex problems, such as optimization and machine learning. This technology is being used to create new AI applications, such as quantum-inspired algorithms for natural language processing and image recognition.
- **Quantum machine learning:** Quantum machine learning is a field of study that explores the use of quantum computing for machine learning applications. It has been used to develop new algorithms for pattern recognition and classification and clustering tasks, as well as to improve existing machine learning algorithms.
- **Quantum neural networks:** Quantum neural networks are a type of artificial neural network that uses quantum computing to process data.

(continued)

These networks have been used to solve complex problems such as image recognition and natural language processing.

- **Quantum natural language processing:** Quantum natural language processing is a field of research that explores the use of quantum computing for natural language processing tasks. It has been used to develop new algorithms that can be used to understand the meaning of text and provide natural language understanding.

- **Quantum image processing:** Quantum image processing is a field of research that explores the use of quantum computing for image processing tasks. It has been used to develop new algorithms that can be used to identify and classify objects.

- **Quantum sensors:** Quantum sensors are being used to measure previously unmeasurable phenomena such as temperature, pressure, magnetic fields, and more, with greater precision and accuracy than ever before.

- **Quantum communications:** Quantum communications are being used to securely transfer information with guaranteed privacy and accuracy.

- **Quantum materials:** Quantum materials are being used to build more efficient, faster, and smaller electronic devices.

- **Quantum cryptography:** Quantum cryptography provides an unbreakable encryption method that can be used to protect sensitive data.

- **Quantum simulation:** Quantum simulations could be used to study complex systems, such as materials for energy applications, and biological systems.

How will AI transform collaborative platforms?

AI will transform collaborative platforms by automating many of the tasks that are typically performed manually by teams. For example, AI-driven tools can be used to analyze conversations and data to identify patterns and trends, suggest solutions to problems, generate reports, and provide personalized recommendations to users. AI-driven bots can also be used to automate mundane tasks such as scheduling meetings, replying to emails, and searching for information. Additionally,

AI can be used to improve security, as AI-driven bots can be used to detect potential security threats and vulnerabilities. AI can also be used to improve the overall user experience on collaborative platforms by providing personalized content and recommendations. AI transformation of collaborative platforms is driving innovation in the enterprise and local business levels by providing the ability to quickly process large amounts of data and automate mundane tasks. For example, AI can be used to automate customer service inquiries, product recommendations, and data analysis. This allows employees to focus on more complex tasks and enables businesses to streamline processes and make better decisions. AI also helps to develop a better understanding of customer preferences and behaviors, which can be used to provide more personalized services and experiences. Additionally, AI can be used to create virtual assistants to help customers navigate their way through the buying process and give businesses the ability to better understand their customers. This can lead to improved customer loyalty and satisfaction. Furthermore, AI can be used to automate marketing and sales processes, allowing businesses to quickly identify the best leads and create more effective campaigns. Finally, by utilizing AI in collaborative platforms, businesses can increase their overall efficiency and productivity.

Some examples:

- **Automated moderation:** AI can be used to detect patterns in user behavior and automatically flag or moderate content that violates a platform's terms of service. This could help ensure that users are adhering to the terms and guidelines of the platform and make it easier for platform administrators to maintain a safe, secure, and productive environment.
- **Natural language processing:** AI can be used to better understand the conversations taking place on collaborative platforms and offer tailored content and recommendations to users. This can make it easier for users to find the content they're looking for and make the platform more engaging.

(continued)

- **Enhanced security:** AI can be used to detect malicious activity on collaborative platforms and alert admins of potential threats. This could help keep users safe and ensure the security of the platform.
- **Automated workflows:** AI can be used to automate processes on collaborative platforms, such as task assignments, user permissions, and other workflow tasks. This can help reduce manual labor and make it easier for admins to manage the platform.
- **Automated meeting summaries:** AI-driven algorithms can automatically generate summaries of team meetings, making it easier for team members to quickly catch up on important updates.
- **Intelligent task assignments:** AI-powered solutions can analyze team member skills and preferences to assign tasks in an optimal way, improving the efficiency and accuracy of task assignments.
- **Automated moderation:** AI-driven moderation tools can help detect and block inappropriate content in real time, making collaborative platforms more safe and secure.
- **Automated translation:** AI-driven translation tools can automatically translate content in different languages, making it easier to collaborate with people from different cultures.
- **AI-driven insights:** AI-based analytics tools can provide insights on team performance and collaboration activities, enabling teams to identify areas for improvement and optimize their workflow.

Digital twins

Digital twins are expected to become even more widely adopted in the future, as the technology continues to develop and become more sophisticated. Organizations will increasingly use digital twins to model and simulate complex systems, leading to improved decision-making, optimization, and cost savings. Digital twin technology is expected to become more widely used in industries such as healthcare, manufacturing, and construction, as well as in smart cities, to improve efficiency and optimize operations. Additionally, digital twins are expected to become more widely used on the Internet of Things (IoT) to create a more connected and dynamic world.

Examples:

■ **Predictive maintenance:** Digital twins can be used to predict when a machine or device is likely to fail, enabling preventive maintenance and reducing downtime.

■ **Automated processes:** Digital twins can be used to automate processes, such as factory automation or autonomous vehicles, by providing the data needed to make decisions and take action.

■ **Smart buildings:** Digital twins can be used to monitor and control building systems such as HVAC, lighting, security, and more.

■ **Smart cities:** Digital twins can be used to improve urban infrastructure, such as traffic control, energy management, and waste management.

Specifically in healthcare:

■ **Real-time monitoring of patient health:** Digital twins can be used to monitor a patient's health in real time by using sensors and medical devices to collect data and analyze it. This data can then be used to generate an accurate representation of the patient's current health status and the potential health risks they face.

■ **Predictive diagnostics:** Digital twins can be used to predict potential health issues before they occur. By using data from medical devices and other sensors, digital twins can detect patterns that may indicate a potential health issue, allowing doctors to intervene and treat the problem before it becomes serious.

■ **Personalized treatment plans:** Digital twins can be used to create personalized treatment plans for patients, based on their specific health needs. By collecting and analyzing data from medical devices and other sources, digital twins can generate individualized plans that are tailored to the patient's specific health needs.

■ **Remote care:** Digital twins can be used to provide remote care to patients. By using data collected from medical devices and other sources, digital twins can provide healthcare professionals with a

(continued)

comprehensive picture of a patient's health, allowing them to provide better care even when the patient is not physically present.

And more specifically in cancer research:

- Using digital twins to simulate and analyze the effects of different treatments and medication combinations on cancer progression.
- Creating digital twins to predict the effectiveness of cancer treatments and investigate the potential risks and benefits of each.
- Utilizing digital twins to simulate the impact of lifestyle factors such as diet, sleep, and exercise on cancer progression.
- Utilizing digital twins to develop personalized treatment plans for individual patients with cancer.
- Studying the impact of environmental factors on cancer progression using digital twins.
- Utilizing digital twins to improve the accuracy of cancer diagnoses and prognoses.
- Developing digital twins to identify cancer biomarkers and develop targeted treatments.
- Utilizing digital twins to simulate cancer progression and test new drugs and treatments in a virtual environment.
- Utilizing digital twins to predict the response of individual patients to different cancer treatments.
- Utilizing digital twins to create predictive models of cancer progression and develop personalized patient care plans.

Next stage for speech recognition, human language processing (and translation), computer vision, and applied methods

Advances in artificial intelligence and natural language processing are enabling machines to better understand and respond to human speech. With the development of more sophisticated algorithms and more powerful hardware, speech recognition and human language processing and translation will become increasingly accurate, efficient, and reliable. In the near future, we can expect machines to become more adept at recognizing and translating spoken conversations, providing a more natural and seamless experience for both humans and machines. Moreover, these technologies will be used to create virtual assistants and bots that can aid in a variety of tasks, from scheduling appointments to providing personalized customer service.

- **Speech recognition:** Natural language understanding (NLU) to enable automated conversations and dialogues.
- **Human language processing (and translation):** Machine learning and deep learning models to better understand and interpret natural language.
- **Computer vision:** Automated image and object recognition to identify and classify objects in images.
- **Applied methods:** Robotic process automation (RPA) to automate repetitive tasks and processes.
- **Improved accuracy:** Speech recognition and human language processing and translation can help improve accuracy and reduce errors in tasks that require human intervention.
- **Cost savings:** Automating tasks through speech recognition and human language processing and translation can help reduce costs associated with manual labor.
- **Increased accessibility:** Speech recognition and human language processing and translation can make tasks more accessible for people with physical or cognitive disabilities.
- **Improved interaction:** Speech recognition and human language processing and translation can help improve user interaction and communication when working with computers.
- **Improved security:** Speech recognition and human language processing and translation can help increase security by allowing for authentication and verification processes.

The Future of Robotics and Humanoids

Robotics and AI are fundamentally transforming humanity's relationship with technology, opening up exciting new possibilities for the future. In many ways, robotics and AI will play a pivotal role in improving our quality of life, solving global problems, automating tedious tasks, protecting the environment, and creating greater opportunities for equity.

Manufacturing offers a particularly promising area for the application of robotics and AI. Robots can take on many of the burdensome, repetitive tasks that humans have traditionally undertaken in factories and warehouses, allowing companies to operate with greater efficiency and lower costs. Additionally, robots can be used in hazardous environments such as mining and construction sites, protecting human workers from dangerous conditions.

In the medical field, robots are increasingly being applied to assist surgeons in performing delicate procedures and delivering care to patients. And in the business world, robots are now being used to complete tasks faster and with fewer errors—some brands are deploying robots for package delivery while others are using them to flip burgers or serve orders.

Robotics and AI also have the potential to significantly improve our quality of life in areas like education, where humanoid robots are helping to personalize learning. And at home, cloud-connected robots can take care of chores such as vacuuming and cooking.

Beyond improving our daily lives, robotics and AI offer an opportunity to solve many of the world's most pressing problems, such as climate change and energy insecurity. They can also help us better understand and protect the natural world around us, creating a more sustainable future for generations to come. Finally, they offer the promise of a more equitable and just society with greater opportunities available to everyone.

It is clear that robotics and AI will play an increasingly integral role in our future. The possibilities are limitless, and we have yet to fully explore all the potential applications these technologies offer.

Bionic Technology Design and Development, from Prosthetic Limbs to Social Empowerment

Robotics and AI have the potential to profoundly shape our world, improving all aspects of life from personal productivity to global sustainability. From prosthetic limbs and exoskeletons that are designed to highlight their technological features to autonomous robots capable of automating tedious tasks, these technologies offer a range of benefits that will improve quality of life and help us build a brighter future for generations to come. They offer the potential of greater equity and opportunity for everyone regardless of their background or circumstances.

Innovations such as Beta Bionics' autonomous bionic pancreas system have already received FDA approval to begin home-use clinical studies, offering hope and excitement for those with Type 1 diabetes. Meanwhile, universities like the University of Central Florida have launched the first US clinical trial of 3D printed prosthetics for children, providing a more affordable alternative to traditional devices and helping children reach their full potential. Such technologies demonstrate not just the benefits bionic technology can bring to individual lives, but, just as importantly, how these breakthroughs can change the way people with physical disabilities are perceived.

Ultimately, robotics and AI have the potential to transform the world for the better by creating new opportunities for everyone—from those living with chronic illnesses to Paralympic athletes competing alongside able-bodied athletes. By embracing innovation and continuing to invest in development, we can ensure that these technologies remain accessible to all and that their potential is fully realized.

From Social Robotics in Classrooms to Supportive Agents in Hospitals

What drives the future of autonomous technology, and how will this impact relations across humanity, economies, and social structures?

The use of robotics and simulators in education provides a wealth of opportunities for students to experience situations that would otherwise be impossible or dangerous. From elementary school through higher education, robotics and simulators offer the ability to bring a "real school" experience to students with severe allergies, practice complex medical procedures without risk, and prepare emergency response and law enforcement trainees for crisis and disaster scenarios.

In elementary and high school, robots are being used to bring students into the classroom who wouldn't be able to attend in person due to severe allergies or other medical conditions. Simulators in driver's education courses provide a true-to-life experience while removing any risk from the scenarios. High school students can learn what it's like to be behind the wheel in a safe classroom environment.

In higher education, robotics are being used in medical instruction to give students a realistic experience of working on human subjects. Students can perform complicated procedures like injections, surgeries, and deliveries through robotics without putting actual people at risk. Simulators offer an all-encompassing environment to practice emergency response and law enforcement scenarios, such as violent altercations or high-speed chases. All of these activities can be experienced with an added level of safety due to the use of simulators.

Overall, robotics and simulators provide real-life experience for students of all ages, preparing them for the real-world scenarios they may encounter in their future careers. The use of robotics and simulators in education creates a safe learning environment for students to explore beyond traditional textbooks and lectures. With their use, students can gain invaluable experience without risk or danger.

How Can We Build Humanoids and Human-Like Robots?

What does it mean to make something that looks and acts like a human? For years, robotics engineers have been trying to create human-like robots that are capable of responding to the world in a manner similar to humans. The aim is to create machines that can learn, think, and act independently and interact with people in ways that make them feel understood.

Recent research has demonstrated that people's perception of a robot depends on how human-like it looks and behaves. For example, researchers at the University of Freiburg in Germany found that when participants watched videos with a human-like robot, they were more likely to rate the robot's actions as intentional rather than programmed, whereas those who interacted with a machine-like robot did not. This suggests that mere exposure to a human-like robot might not be enough to make people believe it is capable of independent thought and emotion, but that human-like behavior might be crucial for being perceived as an intentional agent.

In addition, this research could inform the design of social robots in the future by helping to determine in which contexts social bonding and the attribution of intentionality can be beneficial for the well-being of humans. For example, in elderly care, social bonding with robots might induce a higher degree of compliance with respect to following recommendations regarding taking medication.

Do Machines Have Feelings and Empathy?

The debate around whether machines have feelings and emotions is ongoing, but there are clear signals that artificial intelligence (AI) models like LaMDA possess the potential to achieve consciousness. While many agree that AI models can generate words and phrases based on existing content online, they differ on the interpretation of what those outputs mean. Some believe these outputs signify that the model understands meaning, while others are more skeptical.

What is certain, however, is that AI models like LaMDA need to be managed and monitored closely so they don't produce unintended or harmful outcomes. The case of Blake Lemoine is an example of this kind of oversight in action: his belief in LaMDA's potential sentience was dismissed by Google, showing that the company is taking steps to protect against such risks. Similarly, Emily M. Bender and Timnit Gebru have warned about the dangers of large language models through their research paper.

These examples show how important it is for businesses to ensure they are implementing proper oversight when using AI models. Although there are multiple advantages to using AI, it's important to recognize the potential risks and take steps to mitigate them accordingly. In this way, businesses can make sure they use AI responsibly in order to maximize its potential benefits.

What Is the Role of Social Robotics in Areas of Education and Human Capacity?

As technology continues to advance, the role of robotics in education and human capacity is growing more important. From kindergarten to grade 12, robots are finding their way into classrooms around the world as a tool for teaching and learning. Similarly, social robots are increasingly being used outside of traditional educational settings as a way to foster language development and help people with autism spectrum disorder (ASD) practice important social skills.

For example, language cafés are partnering with robots such as Furhat to provide a perfect, always-patient partner for learning a new language.

In 2018, an initial pilot was conducted in Stockholm using the Furhat robot to help immigrants learn Swedish, and the results were positive. Similarly, social robots can provide a safe, human-like way for children with ASD to practice important skills such as interpreting gestures and different types of social behavior.

Clearly, robotics engineers have made great strides toward achieving the goal of creating robots that look and act like humans. However, there is still much work that needs to be done before robots can truly interact with us in a meaningful way. By understanding the importance of attribution of intentionality and how it can benefit the well-being of humans, robotics engineers can continue to make progress toward this goal. The educational robot market is projected to reach $1,689 million by 2023, which shows that social robotics are increasingly being utilized in areas of education and human capacity. With continued innovation, robots may become more accepted in our lives as providing a form of social interaction.

What Does the Future Look Like for Assistive Robotics and Bionic Technology?

As robotics technology advances, so does the question of how human-like we really want our robots to be. While there are many advantages to having robots that appear and act like humans, such as providing assistance in educational settings and helping those with ASD practice social skills, there is also a fear of confusing, blurred boundaries between human and machine that can be unsettling for some.

This fear is explored by roboticist Dr. Paolo Paladino, who has studied human reactions and attitudes to robots that look increasingly like ourselves. He describes our evolving relationship to these robots as a paradox; on the one hand we want social robots to be human enough in appearance and behavior to fulfill our relationship needs, while on the other hand robots that are "too human" can threaten our sense of human identity and uniqueness.

Building on Paladino's remarks, in order for robots to become fully accepted and integrated into our lives, robotics engineers need to understand the importance of attribution of intentionality and how it can benefit the well-being of humans. This requires an understanding of social cues, emotions, and facial expressions that have long been thought to be exclusive to the human brain but are now being developed by robotics engineers. When it comes to areas like healthcare, education, and assistance, robots can provide a safe and reliable way for humans to interact without the fear of judgment or misunderstanding.

What Role Will Robots Play in Healthcare and Hospitals?

Robotics is playing an increasingly important role in healthcare and hospitals. From robot-assisted surgery to prostheses, robotic exoskeletons, disinfection robots, endoscopic capsules, and robotic nurses—robotics has been used across a wide range of clinical applications. Each of these use cases brings with it various advantages such as reduced blood loss, faster recovery, remarkable user control, and more accurate diagnosis.

However, the introduction of robotics into healthcare is not without its challenges. For instance, clinicians may be wary of machine learning as it involves "black box" models that are difficult to interpret. Consequently, there has been a surge in research related to explainable machine learning to address these concerns. If effective, explainable machine learning will be critical in helping to boost trust in this technology and its use in healthcare decisions.

Robotics also offers an alternative to antibiotics that promises a bright future for healthcare. Nanorobots with receptors can be used to attract bacteria from the bloodstream or local infection sites, thus providing an alternative for antibiotic therapy.

Overall, robotics offers a revolutionary approach to healthcare and hospitals. By streamlining mundane tasks, improving accuracy of diagnosis, and providing alternatives to antibiotics, robotics is revolutionizing how medical care is delivered. The potential applications are limitless and exciting—each offering its own advantages that may one day lead to improved patient outcomes and enhanced quality of life. As such, understanding this technology is critical for any physician looking to incorporate these techniques into their practice.

PART III

Social Impacts of Digital Inclusion

In Part III, we discuss ethics and security concerns, who drives policymaking, and how to ensure that AI is trustworthy. We also work through how AI will affect our everyday lives, from how we speak to how public policy is created.

6

Ethics, Safety, and Security Concerns

Who drives policymaking in artificial intelligence (AI), and how can we ensure that it is ethical? This chapter aims to answer those questions.

The development and implementation of policies related to AI is a complex process that requires collaboration among industry, government, and other stakeholders. AI has the potential to transform our lives in ways both positive and negative, so it is essential that those who create, deploy, and regulate AI ensure that it is developed and used ethically.

At the international level, the OECD's Recommendation of the Council on Artificial Intelligence is a major source of guidance in this area. The United States has been an advocate for this approach and has taken several steps to support its implementation. In 2019, the United States joined together with like-minded democracies of the world in adopting this recommendation, which sets out a series of intergovernmental principles for trustworthy AI. The OECD's Recommendation outlines principles including inclusive growth, human-centered values, transparency, safety and security, and accountability.

The Biden–Harris Administration's Office of Science and Technology Policy also released a blueprint for a "Bill of Rights" in October 2022 to provide guidance on the design, development, and deployment of AI and other automated systems so that they protect the rights of the American public. At the state level, legislation relating to AI was introduced in at least 17 states in 2022, and enacted in Colorado, Illinois, Vermont, and Washington. These measures include creating task forces or commissions to study AI, amending existing laws, and providing funding for the examination of automated decision-making systems.

Ultimately, the ethical use of AI is dependent on an effective policy framework that ensures responsible development and deployment of these technologies. This framework must be driven by a commitment to transparency and accountability, so that stakeholders can understand how decisions are made, and can assess the potential effects of AI on society. By ensuring that policymakers, regulators, and industry work together to create effective policies, we can ensure that AI is used responsibly and equitably for the benefit of all.

Trustworthy AI: Considerations, Use Cases, and Certifications

Imagine a world in which AI is ubiquitous, present in every aspect of our lives from healthcare and transportation to education and entertainment. It's a future that could bring tremendous benefits, but it also exposes us to potential risks such as data privacy, bias, transparency, and more. To ensure that AI technologies are used responsibly, it's essential to establish a framework that takes into account these possible risks and builds trust in these systems.

A critical aspect of this framework is explainable artificial intelligence (XAI). XAI allows humans to better understand and evaluate the outcomes of AI models. It offers insights into model accuracy, fairness, transparency, and outcomes in AI-powered decision-making. This helps organizations build trust in their AI systems and adopt a responsible approach to the development of such technologies.

Consider an analogy of a car. In order to trust a car's safety, it needs to have certain certifications that make sure it follows particular standards for an automobile. It is also important that every part of the car works as expected and does not pose additional risks to its users or environment. Similarly, when implementing AI technologies in an organization, organizations need to make sure they meet certain standards in terms of transparency, accountability, and trustworthiness.

The United States Department of Health and Human Services (HHS) has taken the lead on this issue with the release of the Executive Order on

Maintaining American Leadership in Artificial Intelligence. The order outlines nine principles that agencies must follow when designing, developing, acquiring, and using AI in the federal government. The HHS Office of the Chief Artificial Intelligence Officer (OCAIO) created the Trustworthy AI (TAI) Playbook to help divisions meet this requirement. It consolidates the executive order principles into six trustworthy AI principles.

Organizations can also leverage external certifications to ensure that their AI systems adhere to certain standards. The most widely adopted certification is the International Organization for Standardization (ISO) 37001, which provides a framework that organizations can use to develop and implement an anti-bribery management system. Other certifications such as the American National Standards Institute (ANSI) AI Certification Program also offer organizations a way to demonstrate the trustworthiness of their AI solutions.

The use of explainable AI and certification frameworks are just the first steps toward building trust in AI systems. Organizations must continue to stay up-to-date with advancements in this field, regularly assess the trustworthiness of their models, and ensure that they have an ethical approach to the development and deployment of AI technologies. In doing so, organizations will be better equipped to benefit from AI while mitigating the potential risks associated with this technology.

Where and how do we identify "red" and "stop" lines of AI research, development, and deployment?

What does it mean to draw a line between ethical and unethical AI? One approach is to discuss the broader implications of an AI technology, rather than just its immediate applications. In addition to considering whether a given project has potential for misuse or harm, it's important to look at what could be done with the same set of technologies if used in a different context.

The European Commission's High-Level Expert Group on Artificial Intelligence (HLEG-AI) has developed a set of ethical guidelines for AI development, having identified seven key areas: respect for human autonomy, prevention of harm and discrimination, fairness, transparency and explainability, privacy and data governance, collaborative innovation, and accountability. The guidelines provide a framework for the ethical evaluation of AI, and can serve as a benchmark for companies developing and deploying AI technologies.

The guidelines focus on how to ensure that AI-powered decisions are equitable, safe, and trustworthy, but they also supplement other existing codes of conduct in the tech industry, such as Microsoft's Principles of Responsible Computing and Google's Responsible AI Principles.

Additionally, the directive on ethical aspects of AI recently proposed by the European Commission provides a set of requirements for AI systems based on human rights and fundamental freedoms. The proposal also includes an obligation for developers to assess and mitigate potential risks related to their technologies, as well as provisions for redress and remedies when a system has caused harm.

Ultimately, the responsible use of AI requires us to be proactive in identifying potential ethical dilemmas and potential areas where AI can have negative implications on society. We must also continue to develop standards and guidelines for responsible development and deployment of AI technology, so that we can ensure that AI is used for the benefit of society.

Expert Input and Analysis: How AI Is Positively and Negatively Impacting SDGs

By Vincenzo Aquaro, Chief of Digital Government Branch—Division for Public Institutions and Digital Government—DESA—United Nations

Eight years after the launch of the UN Sustainable Development Goals (SDGs), AI has made significant progress in addressing some of the world's most pressing challenges. While there is still much work to be done, several noteworthy examples illustrate how AI is positively impacting the SDGs.

- **AI for Earth:** Many private sector initiatives harness AI to support projects in agriculture, biodiversity, climate change, and water resources management. AI-driven solutions have improved agricultural yield predictions, wildlife conservation, and climate modeling, directly contributing to SDGs such as Zero Hunger, Climate Action, and Life on Land.

- **AI for Health:** AI has accelerated drug discovery, enabled more accurate diagnosis, and improved healthcare accessibility. For instance, Google's DeepMind developed AlphaFold, which predicts protein structures with unparalleled accuracy, expediting research in areas like drug discovery and disease understanding. Researchers from the University of Bari (Italy) used an AI algorithm of deep machine learning on healthcare data from common medical devices to predict Alzheimer's disease years before doctors can diagnose it. These advancements align with SDG 3, Good Health and Well-being.
- **AI for Education:** Adaptive learning platforms like Knewton and DreamBox utilize AI to deliver personalized learning experiences, helping students improve their performance and bridging educational gaps. By enhancing the quality and inclusivity of education, AI contributes to SDG 4, Quality Education.
- **AI for Renewable Energy:** AI has optimized energy consumption and maximized the efficiency of renewable energy sources. For example, Google's DeepMind reduced the energy used for cooling in data centers by 40% through AI-powered optimization. This supports SDG 7, Affordable and Clean Energy, and SDG 13, Climate Action.

Despite these positive examples, challenges remain. AI's potential to exacerbate social inequalities, enable mass surveillance, and displace jobs highlights the need for responsible AI development that respects human rights and ensures inclusive benefits. Researchers, policymakers, and industry leaders must collaborate to harness AI's potential while minimizing its risks, working toward a future where AI can significantly contribute to achieving the UN SDGs.

How we avoid economic silos and work more holistically within the United Nations framework of the Sustainable Development Goals

To avoid economic silos and work more holistically within the United Nations framework of the SDGs, stakeholders need to

(continued)

adopt an integrated and collaborative approach. Here are some key strategies:

- **Cross-sector collaboration:** Encourage partnerships between governments, the private sector, academia, and civil society to create innovative solutions that address multiple SDGs simultaneously. By working together, stakeholders can leverage their unique expertise and resources for the common goal.
- **Interdisciplinary research:** Promote interdisciplinary research that combines AI and other emerging technologies with fields such as economics, public health, environmental science, and sociology. This approach will lead to more comprehensive solutions that take into account the complexity of global challenges.
- **Policy coherence:** Governments should ensure that their policies align with the SDGs and support the responsible development and deployment of AI. Coherent policies will encourage synergies between different sectors and reduce the risk of unintended consequences.
- **Inclusive technology development:** Prioritize the development of AI solutions that address the needs of marginalized and vulnerable populations. By focusing on inclusivity and equitable access, we can ensure that the benefits of AI are distributed more evenly, helping to reduce inequalities (SDG 10).
- **Capacity building:** Strengthen north–south, south–south, and triangular cooperation to enhance the capacity of developing countries to harness AI and other advanced technologies for sustainable development. This can be achieved through global and regional multi-stakeholder partnerships to mobilize investments in education, infrastructure, and digital skills training, as well as by facilitating technology transfer and knowledge sharing.
- **Monitoring and evaluation:** Establish mechanisms to track the progress of AI initiatives in addressing the SDGs. By collecting data and evaluating outcomes, stakeholders can identify best practices, learn from failures, and adjust strategies as needed.

■ **Ethical considerations:** Incorporate ethical principles and human rights into the design, development, and deployment of AI solutions. By prioritizing transparency, accountability, and fairness, we can minimize potential harms and ensure that AI-driven innovations contribute positively to the SDGs.

By adopting these strategies, stakeholders can work together more holistically within the UN SDG framework, maximizing the potential of AI and other technologies to address global challenges in a sustainable and equitable manner.

How AI and new technologies can contribute to the achievement of the Sustainable Development Goals

AI and new technologies hold great potential for contributing to the achievement of the SDGs by offering innovative solutions, optimizing resources, and enhancing decision-making across various sectors. Here are just few examples in which AI and new technologies can advance all 17 SDGs:

■ **No Poverty (SDG 1):** AI can enhance poverty-alleviation efforts through better targeting of social welfare programs and financial inclusion. Big data and machine learning can identify populations in need, enabling governments and non-governmental organizations (NGOs) to deliver resources more effectively. AI can also support the development of innovative financial services, such as mobile banking, for the unbanked and underbanked.

■ **Agriculture and Food Security (SDG 2):** AI-powered precision agriculture tools enable better crop management, pest control, and yield predictions, helping to improve food production and reduce waste. Satellite imagery combined with machine learning algorithms can monitor land use, track deforestation, and support sustainable agriculture practices.

■ **Health and Well-being (SDG 3):** AI-driven diagnostics, telemedicine, and drug discovery can revolutionize healthcare. AI can

(continued)

identify patterns in medical data, leading to more accurate diagnoses and personalized treatments. Telemedicine, powered by AI, can expand access to healthcare services in remote and underserved areas.

- **Education and Skills (SDG 4):** AI-based adaptive learning platforms can deliver personalized learning experiences, identifying knowledge gaps and adjusting content based on individual needs. AI can also help educators develop targeted interventions and monitor student progress, fostering inclusive and equitable education.

- **Gender Equality (SDG 5):** AI-driven analysis of gender-related data can help identify and address gaps in gender equality, such as pay disparities and workplace discrimination. AI tools can also assist in raising awareness about gender issues, as well as in the development of targeted policies and programs that promote gender equality.

- **Clean Water and Sanitation (SDG 6):** AI can optimize water management by predicting water demand, identifying leaks, and enhancing wastewater treatment. Additionally, AI can monitor water quality in real time, enabling early detection of contamination and supporting sustainable water resource management.

- **Affordable and Clean Energy (SDG 7):** AI can optimize energy consumption in buildings, transportation, and industry, while maximizing the efficiency of renewable energy sources. AI-driven smart grids can balance energy supply and demand, reducing waste and facilitating the integration of renewable energy into existing systems.

- **Decent Work and Economic Growth (SDG 8):** AI can increase productivity by automating repetitive tasks and assisting in decision-making processes. AI-driven tools can identify skills gaps and help develop targeted workforce training programs, preparing workers for the future labor market. AI can also improve workplace safety by predicting and preventing accidents.

- **Industry, Innovation, and Infrastructure (SDG 9):** AI can drive innovation by accelerating research and development in various industries. AI-powered predictive maintenance can reduce downtime and increase efficiency in industrial processes. Additionally,

AI can support the development of sustainable infrastructure by optimizing design, construction, and resource management.

- **Reduced Inequalities (SDG 10):** AI can help identify patterns of inequality and discrimination, enabling policymakers to develop targeted interventions. AI-powered tools can facilitate equal access to opportunities, such as job-matching platforms that reduce bias in hiring processes. However, it is crucial to ensure that AI systems are designed and deployed fairly to avoid exacerbating existing inequalities. To do so, AI should work as an equalizer for inclusion, and different approaches that integrate multilevel, multisectoral, and multidisciplinary strategies should be adopted to insure the principle of "inclusion by design."

- **Sustainable Cities and Communities (SDG 11):** AI and new technologies can contribute significantly to achieving this goal, which focuses on making cities and human settlements inclusive, safe, resilient, and sustainable, in various ways. One notable example is in urban planning and smart cities. Moreover, AI-driven systems can help monitor and manage urban energy consumption, waste management, and air quality. For example, AI can optimize waste collection routes, reducing fuel consumption and emissions, while smart sensors can detect air pollution and inform mitigation strategies. In the context of smart cities, AI and Internet of Things (IoT) technologies can improve urban mobility by optimizing traffic management and public transportation systems. For instance, AI algorithms can predict traffic congestion, enabling better traffic flow and reducing greenhouse gas emissions. Autonomous vehicles, guided by AI, can further contribute to reduced congestion and improved road safety.

- **Responsible Consumption and Production (SDG 12):** AI can enhance resource efficiency and waste management by optimizing production processes, reducing waste, and improving recycling systems. AI can also support the development of circular economies through the analysis of consumption patterns and identification of opportunities for resource recovery.

(continued)

- **Climate Action (SDG 13):** AI can improve climate modeling, enabling more accurate predictions and facilitating better adaptation and mitigation strategies. AI-powered platforms can track greenhouse gas emissions, support sustainable transportation planning, and optimize supply chains to minimize environmental impact.
- **Life Below Water (SDG 14):** AI can monitor and predict changes in marine ecosystems, enabling better conservation and management strategies. AI-driven tools can identify illegal fishing activities, track marine pollution, and support the development of sustainable aquaculture practices.
- **Sustainable Development Goal 15 (SDG 15):** AI can play a crucial role in achieving this goal, which aims to protect, restore, and promote sustainable use of terrestrial ecosystems, halt biodiversity loss, and combat desertification, by aiding in conservation efforts and monitoring ecosystems. One notable example is the use of AI for wildlife conservation. AI-powered tools can analyze data from camera traps, drones, and satellite imagery to monitor wildlife populations and their habitats. Machine learning algorithms can automatically identify and track individual animals or species, providing valuable insights into their distribution, behavior, and the threats they face, such as poaching or habitat loss.
- **Peace, Justice, and Strong Institutions (SDG 16):** AI can support the rule of law and justice by automating legal research, identifying patterns in crime data, and improving public safety. AI-driven tools can enhance government transparency and accountability by monitoring corruption and promoting open data initiatives.
- **Partnerships for the Goals (SDG 17):** AI can foster global partnerships by facilitating knowledge sharing and technology transfer. AI-driven platforms can connect stakeholders, enabling collaborations across sectors and countries to address global challenges collectively.

These are just a few, as the huge potentialities of the integration of responsible AI and new cutting-edge technologies into various sectors can drastically accelerate progress toward the SDGs and create a more sustainable and equitable future for all.

How Does AI Affect Rights, Meanings, Vocabulary, and Relationships?

Ask yourself this: How does AI affect our rights, meanings, vocabulary, and relationships? It might seem like an abstract concept, but AI has the capacity to significantly shape these aspects of life. Through the use of coding and algorithms, AI can "regulate" in ways that traditional laws cannot. This new form of regulation is called "regulation by code" and it allows for rules to be enforced ex-ante (before people act) as opposed to ex-post (after the fact). The majority of people without technical knowledge or resources have no choice but to comply with the code, which makes AI a powerful tool for regulation.

At the same time, AI also has the potential to improve communication and understanding by making vocabulary more inclusive. For example, Microsoft 365 subscribers can now opt to see suggestions for inclusive language that seek to eliminate biases based on gender, age, ability, and more. Specifically, a new feature of Microsoft Word's Editor is that it can use AI to offer suggestions for rewriting full sentences rather than offering spelling or grammar fixes one at a time, which is nearly 15% more effective than previous methods in catching mistakes. By catching errors commonly made by those with dyslexia and offering whole-sentence rewrite suggestions to improve fluency, conciseness, and readability, AI helps ensure that messages are understood in their intended way.

Regardless of the potential benefits, several ethical questions arise from the increasing reliance on AI to regulate and communicate. How do we ensure that data sets used to train AI systems are not biased? Who has the right to control and decide how personal data is collected and used by companies? And ultimately, who holds responsibility when something goes wrong with an AI system?

To answer these questions, we must continue to research and analyze the implications of AI as a regulatory technology. Primavera De Filippi and Samer Hassan have suggested that this new form of regulation is pushing us into a world where "Law Is Code,"[1] making it necessary for us to gain an understanding of these technologies in order to ensure their responsible use.

Therefore, the way forward is to create a balance between the advantages that AI can bring, such as more accurate communication, and the risks posed by its use in terms of privacy, bias, data ownership, and accountability. As AI continues to become more embedded in our lives, understanding how it influences our rights, meanings, vocabulary, and relationships is essential for building a better future.

AI for Trusted and Resilient Public Services

The ever-increasing complexity of the global economic landscape has driven the need for trusted and resilient public services, especially considering the heightened security threats in today's digital world. With the emergence of AI, questions have risen as to whether this technology can be reliably employed in public sector operations.

In response to this, governments are increasingly turning to AI as a powerful tool for improving the performance of public services and ensuring their trustworthiness. AI-enabled systems can quickly process large data sets to provide a more holistic picture of both citizen needs and available resources. This helps policymakers create better-informed and evidence-based policy initiatives that are tailored to meet the needs of citizens. AI can also be used to help ensure resilience in public services by enabling agencies to quickly and efficiently identify, respond to, and address unforeseen events or challenges.

This section explores the potential benefits of harnessing AI for public services, with specific focus on how it can be used to improve decision-making, eliminate bias, and enable resilience in operations.

Expert Input and Analysis: AI Helps Both Business and Governments Model for a More Resilient Future

By Kay Firth-Butterfield, Executive Director, Centre for Trustworthy Technology, a World Economic Forum Centre for the Fourth Industrial Revolution, former Head of Artificial Intelligence and a member of the Executive Committee of the World Economic Forum

I think that climate adaptation using AI has been neglected in favor of mitigation, but this year [2022] it was brought forward. There are so many potentially valuable ways in which AI can help both business and governments model for a more resilient future. Of course, this can only happen with good governance around the use of AI. Therefore, I am delighted to see more and more companies appointing Responsible AI teams in-house or reaching out for good advice.

With generative AI exploding in 2022 and starting to be used by companies, in 2023 those companies need to be careful. Generative AI suffers from all the problems we have identified in AI and some more that unwary users might not suspect, for example the court cases around the use of IP/copyrighted material. As AI learns more and makes fewer errors we might believe that AI has achieved human intelligence, but it behooves us to remember that however smart they appear, what is happening is prediction of the next word in a sentence, not deep thought. The time is truly now for humanity to decide and design its future with AI.

How we ensure that those currently in charge of policymaking in AI create policies and guidelines that are ethical

Currently the world is politically and economically fragmented. It's impossible to have agreed solutions for any uses of AI. There has been an effort at the UN level by some of the most important academics in AI to get lethal autonomous weapons banned outright. Surprisingly, or perhaps not, Russia and the United States are opposed to such a ban.

The mindset of politicians in Europe varies considerably from those in the United States, so Europe is pushing ahead with the EU AI Act, which takes a risk-based approach to AI. High-risk uses will be banned and many would say that this approach follows that of most ethical listings of concerns about uses of AI, for example, facial recognition technology. In the United States there has been a Bill of Rights pertaining to AI and a careful NIST [National Institute of Standards and Technology] report setting out recommendations for the responsible use of AI, but no federal law. However, state governments have been passing laws, resulting in more fragmentation that makes it hard for businesses. As with all things, to achieve ethical approaches to law we, the citizens, must take an active part in our democracy.

However, that brings me to the billions who not only do not live in a democracy but also do not have access to the Internet, let alone AI. It is this growing north–south divide that should be of great concern, especially with the growth of LLMs [large language models] that

(continued)

create new content from a web that doesn't portray the cultures and achievements of all.

Trustworthy AI use cases

I sit on the board of EarthSpecies. Our aim is to use AI to help us understand nonhuman languages. This is truly first contact but with a species that have been living on earth longer than us, whales. What we hope is that by enabling us to understand them we will give them, and our fellow animals, a voice at the table to discuss our stewardship of the planet.

This is not to say that they will actually engage in conversations, but we know that when women and other oppressed groups were given a voice, change for the better happened. The AI we design is used to exacting ethical standards and we are currently working on creating a Responsible AI roadmap for our interactions with another species, which cannot protect itself.

AI and the World Economic Forum: a glimpse of the future

My team and I work tirelessly and with passion to ensure that everyone will have a prosperous, healthy, and rewarding life in the age of AI. We have created tools that any business, large or small, can use to ensure that they can introduce rigorous processes to design, develop, and use AI responsibly.

Likewise, we have open source tools for governments to adopt in transformation, using AI in a trustworthy fashion and meeting the civil and human rights of their citizens. I regularly host a podcast (*Tech and Ethics*) that is designed to enable practitioners of Responsible AI to learn from one another and we have collaborated with many stakeholders from business, government, academia, and the nonprofit sector to create and open source tools using AI which can predict where wildfires will start before they do. This ground-breaking work shows the true potential of AI to solve some of our greatest challenges, but only if used in an ethical way.

AI leveraged to help humans speak to whales?

Whales communicate with each other through complex vocalizations, and these vocalizations are specific to each species and can carry a range of meanings.

Some researchers are exploring the use of AI and machine learning to analyze whale vocalizations and develop a better understanding of how these vocalizations are used for communication. For example, they are developing algorithms to identify different whale species based on their vocalizations and to classify the different types of sounds they produce.

Additionally, there have been some attempts to use AI to translate human speech into sounds that are more easily recognizable to whales. This involves analyzing the acoustic properties of human speech and modifying it to create sounds that are more similar to whale vocalizations.

Although these efforts are still in the early stages, AI has the potential to help us better understand and communicate with these intelligent creatures. However, it is important to note that communicating with whales is a complex task, and it may take many years of research and development before AI can be used effectively to facilitate communication with these animals.

There have been a number of research projects exploring the use of AI to communicate with whales. Here are some examples:

- **Project CETI:** The Cetacean Translation Initiative (CETI) is a project that aims to develop a language translation system for communicating with dolphins and whales. The project is using machine learning algorithms to analyze and classify the vocalizations of dolphins and whales in order to develop a database of whale sounds that can be translated into human speech.
- **OceanMind:** OceanMind is a nonprofit organization that uses AI and machine learning to combat illegal fishing. The organization uses satellite data to monitor fishing vessels, and AI algorithms to analyze the data and identify vessels engaged in illegal fishing activities.

(continued)

■ **Deep Sea Mining Campaign:** The Deep Sea Mining Campaign is a nonprofit organization that is using AI to monitor the impacts of deep-sea mining on marine wildlife. The organization is using machine learning algorithms to analyze satellite data and monitor changes in the ocean environment, including changes in whale vocalizations.

■ **Marine Mammal Monitoring:** Marine Mammal Monitoring is a project that uses AI to detect and identify whale and dolphin vocalizations in real time. The system uses machine learning algorithms to analyze acoustic data and identify the species of whale or dolphin that is vocalizing.

These examples demonstrate the potential of AI and machine learning to help us better understand and communicate with whales and other marine wildlife. However, more research and development is needed to fully realize the potential of these technologies in this area.

AI Can Support Evidence-Based Policymaking

Uncertainty and ambiguity are pervasive in the public sector, making it difficult to discern if a given policy is actually achieving its desired outcome. Think of it as a game of whack-a-mole; state and local policymakers are often able to clearly articulate the goals and objectives of a given agency, but have difficulty knowing which actions taken by those departments are actually achieving the prescribed outcomes. Questions like "what works?" and "for whom?" are nearly impossible to answer without data-driven evidence.

The good news is that artificial intelligence (AI) can provide the data-rich insights necessary to ensure that public services are consistently meeting their predetermined objectives. AI-based models can be used to test, iterate, and refine programs in order to improve decision-making based on evidence rather than guesswork. The London School of Economics found that only 4.5% of over 15,000 national, state, and local programs were adequately evaluated to ensure their effectiveness; with the help of AI, governments can begin to close this gap.

AI-based models are also useful for predicting when and where future interventions may be needed and for whom, while identifying errors or mistakes that allow human operators to course correct. These models can also serve as a check on human bias or misinformation. This chapter dives deeper into these topics, and the belief that beyond the ability to improve the quality of decision-making, AI systems offer several other benefits to policymaking.

Humans are meant to lead, not follow. AI systems should be used to support public sector decision-makers and help them gain more granular insights into how their programs are performing. This will enable state and local governments to build better trust with citizens by providing data-driven evidence of the effectiveness of their policies.

AI Requires Communities and Policymakers to Explicitly Define Values

Consider a parable of two roads diverging in a wood: one leading to a city with ample public coffers, and the other leading to an underfunded township. In both instances, policymakers must make decisions on how they prioritize investments in road work by analyzing traffic bottlenecks. The problem is the same but the values differ: in a city with ample public coffers, policymakers may prioritize reducing false positives—spending money on roads that don't need repairs—over false negatives. In an underfunded township, however, they may prefer to prioritize missed bottlenecks over wasting resources.

This illustrates why it is essential for communities and policymakers to explicitly define their values when working with AI. Artificial intelligence has the potential to accelerate the analysis of large amounts of data, identify patterns, and generate insights in near-real time—all while taking into account contextual factors such as historical practices and regional differences—but only if it is programmed with its values at the start.

In Australia, the Victoria State Government's "syndromic surveillance program," for example, successfully identified six public health concerns within four months of being implemented. Crucially, it was designed to do this by taking into account the values and needs of its users. Similarly, in Quebec, economic development specialists are leveraging AI tools to develop a more-nuanced understanding of subregions, but only by explicitly accounting for values and needs at the start. Moreover, in New Orleans, an emergency services agency was able to optimize the placement of

ambulances closest to where they were most needed by equipping its algorithms with values that took into account historical practices. Specifically,
it designed its algorithms to account for practices that had previously pre-
vented poor neighborhoods from receiving faster services.

The success of all these projects is a testament to the fact that AI
requires communities and policymakers to explicitly define values in order
to ensure successful implementation. Only then can they ensure that their
AI-powered solutions generate the desired outcomes.

Global Cooperation

The Latin word for "cooperate" is "cooperari," which translates to "working
together." This may be the most apt way to explain how global cooperation
and multi-stakeholder approaches are paramount in today's interconnected
world. The increasing complexity of risk, from climate change and cyber
threats, can no longer be met by one single stakeholder. Therefore, it is
essential for governments, businesses, academia, and civil society to work
together as a part of a multi-stakeholder approach. This section looks at
several examples of multi-stakeholder cooperatives, which are organizations
that involve actors from different sectors in the supply chain and other areas,
and provide commentary on the importance of global cooperation and
multi-stakeholder approaches.

We also discuss AI policy frameworks and the role of the G20 and the
OECD in multi-stakeholder dialogue.

First, it is paramount to discuss the United Nations Sustainable Development Goals (SDGs) and their role in global cooperation. The SDGs are a
set of 17 goals created to serve as a blueprint on how to create a better and
more sustainable world by 2030. Specifically, the SDGs include topics such
as ending poverty, reducing inequality, and promoting peace and justice.
Artificial intelligence is not included as part of the 17 goals. However, it is
important to discuss the role of AI in accelerating the SDGs. AI can be used
to monitor environmental threats, analyze data for better decision-making
for complex problems such as food insecurity and poverty, and can also
facilitate cross-border collaboration.

- **Environmental threats:** AI can be used to track global air, water,
  and soil quality. AI-based sensors can detect leaks of toxic materials

or pollutants, allowing for early warning systems to be created to protect humans and the environment.

- **Data analysis:** By analyzing data on poverty and food insecurity, AI can help governments understand which areas are most vulnerable to poverty and come up with innovative solutions to alleviate poverty and hunger.
- **Cross-border collaboration:** AI can facilitate cross-border collaboration by connecting stakeholders from different countries who share similar objectives. This could lead to more efficient decision-making and improved results.

There are several key examples of multi-stakeholder cooperatives that are working toward the SDGs and exemplify the importance of global cooperation.

- **The Fifth Season Cooperative** is a regional food hub that aggregates and distributes locally grown produce, meats, dairy, and value-added products throughout the greater Driftless Area in the Midwest. This cooperative has six member classes that span the entire supply chain from producers, producer groups, processors, distributors, buyers, and workers. This type of cooperative benefits the local economy while encouraging sustainability through its model of collaboration among all stakeholders.
- **Weaver Street Market** is a multi-stakeholder cooperative grocery store in North Carolina that has been in operation since 1988. The organization offers both consumer and worker memberships and is often described as "a grocery store with a conscience." It is committed to local and organic foods, sustainability, and fair trade practices.
- **The Global Alliance for Trade Facilitation (GATF)** based in Colombia is another example of multi-stakeholder cooperation, bringing together the private sector, government, and civil society to help promote global trade. Through the GATF, INVIMA, Colombia's National Food and Drug Surveillance Institute, is helping to implement a modern risk-management system. This system will help create more secure trading environments for both domestic and international companies. GATF includes the likes of the World Economic Forum and is a testament to how ubiquitous collaboration can be in modern-day business operations. The organization also

helps create a level playing field for businesses by removing barriers to trade and encouraging transparency and accountability with regard to international business rules.

- **The Friends of Climate Action** initiative, governed by the World Economic Forum, is tackling global climate change through the use of multi-stakeholder collaboration. This forum brings together businesses, investors, and civil society to work collectively toward ambitious action plans that aid in mitigating risks associated with climate change. By providing a platform for these entities to connect, they are able to exchange ideas and develop more effective measures to address the issue. The Forum also serves as an advocate for global collaboration and encourages further participation from different stakeholders in order to achieve a wider impact. Friends of Climate Action is an example of how multiple parties can work together to produce meaningful change on a global scale.

- **The Financial Services Information Sharing and Analysis Center (FS-ISAC)** is another example of multi-stakeholder collaboration in action. This organization works together with the US government to provide cyberthreat assessments and alerts to its members, which are typically financial companies. FS-ISAC's efforts not only help businesses stay informed of imminent threats but also offer recommended solutions that can be put into place for further risk mitigation. Its work highlights the significance of public–private collaboration in tackling cybersecurity risks, and its success serves as evidence that such partnerships can be immensely beneficial. Through initiatives like FS-ISAC, we are seeing how multi-stakeholder collaborations are playing an increasingly important role in global risk management efforts.

Moreover, the G20 and the OECD are two of the most important international organizations that support global cooperation and multi-stakeholder approaches.

- **G20:** Through the G20, leaders of 19 countries and the European Union come together to discuss global economic issues. The group was founded in 1999 in order to promote international cooperation and foster sustainable growth in the global economy. To ensure comprehensive input, the G20 actively engages a diverse group of stakeholders through their Engagement Groups (B20, L20, C20, T20, W20, Y20 and U20) in multi-stakeholder dialogue aimed at developing global solutions. These groups represent business, labor, civil society, think tanks, youth, and academia, respectively.

- **OECD:** The Organisation for Economic Co-operation and Development (OECD) is an international economic organization of 37 countries, founded in 1961 to stimulate economic progress and world trade. It works to build better policies for better lives by promoting economic growth, providing employment opportunities, improving living standards, and investing in human capital. As a forum of countries committed to democracy and the market economy, it provides a platform to compare policy experiences, seek answers to common problems, identify good practices, and coordinate the domestic and international policies of its members. The OECD is also at the forefront of efforts to understand and tackle major global challenges such as climate change, development and poverty reduction, and international terrorism. Its publications provide economic analysis and statistics to member countries, while its committees and working parties examine specific policy issues in depth. The OECD also works with developing countries to help them build better economic systems and reduce poverty. Through its international development assistance programs, it provides technical advice, assistance, and training for governments of developing countries and facilitates their integration into the global economy.

In conclusion, the role of multi-stakeholder collaboration in tackling global challenges is growing increasingly important. From initiatives such as Friends of Climate Action and the FS-ISAC to organizations like the G20 and OECD, we are seeing firsthand how partnerships between different stakeholders can be leveraged to create meaningful change on a global scale. Building on this, the following chapter explores the ecosystem and investment approach to AI adoption that organizations should consider in order to ensure a successful transition into an AI-driven world. It is clear that organizations need to take a strategic, comprehensive view of their efforts instead of just focusing on technological solutions if they want to successfully adopt artificial intelligence. The next chapter explores how to do just that.

Expert Input and Analysis: Sustainable Development Goals and the Greatest Existential Risks That Humanity Face

By Robert Opp, Chief Digital Officer, UNDP

Unfortunately, the COVID-19 pandemic has set us back quite a bit in terms of human development and Sustainable Development Goals (SDGs). However, at the same time we see incredible potential for the growing power of technologies like artificial intelligence to help accelerate our progress and get us back on track. That includes the issue of sustainability, which is obviously one of the greatest existential risks that humanity faces right now. Both in terms of mitigation as well as adaptation, we believe the power of technology can be harnessed to protect people and our planet.

How we avoid economic silos and work on the UN Framework with UN SDGs collaboratively across industries

Global collaboration on AI, across the public and private sectors, is essential to ensure the highest standards for human rights–based, inclusive, and ethical deployment of AI, in line with the international rules and regulations.

The silos we face aren't just economic or industry-based. Different countries have distinct national strategies and interests, legal traditions, economic systems, demographics, and geographies. So the situation is complex.

However, on the positive side we believe that effective international cooperation doesn't necessarily have to mean global harmonization. International cooperation can be structured in a way that enables countries and other players to participate in a productive competition and cooperation in AI—a kind of "coopetition"—that includes agreeing on a set of fundamental principles and seeking joint action and outputs, but also allowing for competition among the best solutions to be scaled.

We need to work on a few of the fundamentals that would underpin global cooperation on AI. One of the most important for us is to ensure that AI is inclusive and puts people and their rights at the center when it comes to data sets, design, and implementation. We can't expect AI systems to serve all people or the whole planet well if we are not including perspectives from everyone. In addition, we need to make sure the processes, algorithms, and decision-making systems are transparent and understandable to all stakeholders as well. This will all help to ensure that AI technologies are ethical, fair, and aligned with the values and principles of the SDGs.

Another important area we need to work on is getting policies and regulations right. Data is at the core of any AI system, and we need to help foster a culture of data sharing and interoperability with strong governance systems that protect people's privacy to ensure that AI technologies are accessible to all, and to facilitate the development of new and innovative solutions. At the same time, we need to ensure that harms caused through AI systems are investigated and addressed, by enacting strong enforcement mechanisms and remedial actions, to make certain that human rights and fundamental freedoms and the rule of law are respected.

Finally, I think that it is important to look at how we can build platforms for international cooperation on AI that support the SDGs by sharing and pooling digital commons, or digital public goods. This might take the form of data commons, reusable proven technology solutions, domain knowledge, or infrastructure. These could be freely available to all to use and accelerate digital progress. The challenge to overcome with this idea is how to sustain and evolve these public goods with financing and support overall.

How we ensure that governments do not work in silos

For AI policy cooperation, exchange between countries on AI policies, data governance, and institutional preparedness measures is critical. The UN is actually already facilitating global discussions on AI and developing guiding principles, frameworks, tools, and mechanisms through which global cooperation on AI can be strengthened.

(continued)

UN member states have an opportunity over the next couple of years to work on these issues. The UN Secretary-General has called for a Summit of the Future in September 2024 that will take up a number of critical global issues, including AI, in a "Global Digital Compact" to be agreed upon among member states. The Compact is expected to help establish shared principles and common platforms around the use and governance of AI in favor of people and the planet.

The UN system, of course, is already active as well to work on common principles and frameworks. For example, an UN Inter Agency Working Group on AI (led by UNESCO and ITU) has worked collaboratively to define the very first global standard-setting instrument on the ethical and responsible use of AI. In November 2021, the 193 Member States at UNESCO's General Conference adopted the Principles on the Ethics of Artificial Intelligence. This will not only protect and promote human rights and human dignity, but will also be an ethical guiding compass and a global normative bedrock allowing the building of strong respect for the rule of law in the digital world.

The AI & Global Governance platform, launched by the United Nations University Center of Policy and Research, will add a unique value to existing debates on ethical AI and AI policies by addressing questions of high relevance, not only to AI practitioners and policymakers, but also to multilateralism. The platform's goal is to combine AI and policy expertise with real-world learning. The platform will bring together a diverse community of leaders and policymakers interested in debating and interacting with the ethical risks, AI policies, and possibilities that have arisen as a result of the AI revolution.

Leaders and policymakers must collaborate

Top-level leaders and policymakers within government should work together to develop an effective plan that aligns technological decisions with the overall country vision and incorporates both technical and managerial viewpoints, drawing on experiences acquired from previous technology changes.

The lack of planning between leaders and policymakers, as well as a lack of resources, all too frequently create an environment in which policies and practices are developed and implemented without a clear grasp of how to assess their effectiveness. To generate more value and influence from AI systems, leaders must engage with policymakers to define a cyclical multi stage process of identification, formulation, adoption, implementation, and evaluation. (Refer to UNESCO's publication "AI and Education: Guidance for Policy-makers.")

UNDP will be launching an "AI Readiness Assessment" tool, which takes an inclusive, whole-of-society approach to assessing the readiness of governments both as a user of AI technologies and as an enabler. This tool can help leaders and policymakers align around a common blueprint for action, and develop inclusive AI policies based on global best practices.

7 | An Ecosystem and Investment Approach to AI Adoption

How can we make AI practical and accessible? This chapter aims to answer that question.

When something is described as practical and accessible, it often means that there are few barriers to entry and the process is not overly complex. For AI to become practical and accessible, we need to focus on ways of making it easier to use, reducing costs associated with developing and using AI technology, and creating an equitable environment that encourages diverse perspectives.

One proposed approach to reduce the complexity of AI development and make it more accessible is through no-code or low-code platforms. These platforms allow developers to create applications quickly, with minimal coding. This approach has been adopted by many tech giants, including Amazon with its Honeycode platform. This type of technology opens up

129

opportunities for companies that may not have access to traditional development resources or expertise.

Another approach is to reduce the amount of data and computing power needed to develop an AI application. Founded by Rachel Thomas and Jeremy Howard, Fast.ai has developed a training technique that can allow applications to be built with just 30 data points, without needing expensive computing power. Moreover, the cost of access to a cloud-based GPU has been reduced to just 45 cents per hour. This type of technology helps reduce the cost and complexity of AI development, allowing developers more access and flexibility when it comes to testing and development. This lowers the barrier for entry into developing AI applications and allows those with limited resources to get involved.

Finally, it is important that AI reflects the diverse perspectives of its users. Increased diversity within the development and use of AI can help reduce or eliminate problems such as bias and unfairness. This can be achieved by encouraging more people from different backgrounds to get involved in developing and using AI technologies, through programs like those offered by Fast.ai. This will help ensure that AI is representing the interests of all users, not just those from privileged backgrounds.

Helping AI Communities and Ecosystems to Thrive

At its core, an ecosystem is a balanced and living system in which the components work together and interact with each other to create a healthy environment. AI communities are no different—in order for them to thrive, they need to be open and accessible to everyone, have access to high-quality data sets, foster collaboration between stakeholders, and promote diversity at all levels of development.

According to Gartner, 85% of AI projects will fail due to biases in data, algorithms, or the teams responsible for managing them.[1] This is due to the fact that many AI projects lack diversity in terms of team composition and data sets. To help address this issue, companies should strive to create a diverse development team—one that is representative of all groups of people—and use data sets that are comprehensive, privacy-compliant, and free of bias.

Bias can be defined as a form of prejudice or discrimination in which people are treated differently based on membership in a certain group. AI bias can manifest itself in many different forms, including gender and racial bias. To combat this, companies should support science, technology, engineering, and math (STEM) education and mentor women for leadership roles to help promote gender diversity. This will ensure that everyone has the opportunity to take part in the development of AI technologies, regardless of gender.

For example, the Girl Scouts of America has been working to empower young women by providing them with access to STEM education and mentorship. They are also collaborating with industry leaders in order to prepare these women to become future AI leaders.

In addition, companies should foster collaboration between stakeholders and promote open dialogue around issues such as privacy, data ethics, and accountability. This will ensure that all stakeholders understand the importance of addressing bias in AI and work together to ensure that AI solutions are both ethical and effective.

By creating an environment that is open and accessible to everyone, fostering collaboration between stakeholders, and promoting diversity at all levels of development, companies will be able to build trust and confidence in their AI solutions while also creating an inclusive ecosystem that can help advance the development of AI technologies and ensure its positive impact on society. This will create a more equitable future for everyone involved in the AI ecosystem.

Building Feasible AI Businesses, Technologies, and Solutions Globally

According to a 2021 survey by McKinsey, AI adoption is on the rise globally, with 56% of respondents reporting that AI has been adopted in at least one function.[2] This figure is highest in emerging economies such as China and India, where 57% of respondents reported adoption. However, only 8% of firms are engaging in core practices to support widespread AI adoption—a figure that is unacceptably low.

The snail-like progress of AI initiatives isn't due to a lack of technology and talent, but to the inability to realign company culture, structure, and ways of working to accommodate AI. This requires an organization-wide commitment that not only embraces AI, but also rewires the company's processes and mindsets in order to maximize its potential.

Organizational change starts with leadership, and leaders must provide clear direction and create a supportive environment to encourage adoption of AI. Companies should aim to build interdisciplinary teams that take on initiatives jointly, as this helps ensure synergy between different departments when leveraging AI solutions. Leaders should also empower front-line employees by introducing data-driven decision-making at the front line, enabling them to make autonomous decisions and trust the algorithms' suggestions.

For AI initiatives to be successful, companies must also embrace a culture of experimentation. To do this, they will have to become more agile and flexible while still managing risk effectively. By creating an environment that encourages employees to take risks in pursuit of creative solutions, enterprises can foster an environment of innovation that allows them to explore new ideas and push boundaries.

For example, a company can set up an internal incubator or innovation lab that develops ideas and technologies with broad implications for the organization. These labs can be used to test new AI applications, explore ways of using analytics and machine learning effectively, and experiment with various business models.

Finally, businesses must prioritize open communication about AI initiatives throughout the organization. They should provide education on the current and future implications of AI, creating a shared vision that encourages employees to become part of the journey. This will ensure that everyone understands why AI is important to the business and how they can contribute.

An easy way to start is by establishing an AI council, a cross-functional team of representatives from various parts of the business that can discuss and review current initiatives. By engaging stakeholders in this way, companies can ensure that everyone is on the same page when it comes to implementing AI solutions. Another solution is to create a central repository of resources and guidelines for AI initiatives. This will help ensure that everyone has the same level of information on upcoming projects and can understand how their work impacts these initiatives.

By implementing these strategies, businesses can successfully build feasible AI solutions that are embraced by the whole organization. With clear direction from leadership, interdisciplinary collaboration, a culture of experimentation, and open communication about AI initiatives, companies can unlock the power of AI to transform their businesses.

Catalyzing AI Communities to Share Solutions Around the World

An ecosystem is only as strong as its members. As AI technology continues to rapidly evolve, it's essential that communities from around the globe come together to share best practices and create real-world solutions. Fortunately, cross-border cooperation is increasingly commonplace in the AI space, with initiatives like the European Union's "AI for Good" program bringing together researchers and policymakers to advance progress in areas such as public health, nature and society, climate and energy, accessibility, and crisis response.

In Latin America, there are a variety of organizations that focus on AI-related research and development. Nodos, a network of Latin American laboratories on artificial intelligence, has been established to foster collaboration between the various countries in the region. In addition, organizations such as Mexico's Instituto Tecnológico de Estudios Superiores (ITESM) have set up Applied AI Laboratories to help promote and facilitate knowledge-sharing between countries.

In Africa, the African Union has launched the African Artificial Intelligence Alliance (AAIA) to ensure sustainable development across the continent through AI. The alliance is made up of a range of public- and private-sector organizations, including universities, research institutions, corporate entities, civil society groups, and public agencies. The AAIA is committed to promoting the use of AI for economic, social, and environmental development in Africa.

In Asia, countries like China and India have taken a leading role in driving the growth of AI on the continent. In particular, Chinese companies such as Tencent and Alibaba are investing heavily in developing their own AI-related technologies and services. Meanwhile, India has made significant investments to develop a comprehensive AI ecosystem, with initiatives such as the National Artificial Intelligence Mission (NAIM) aiming to promote AI-driven growth across a range of sectors including agriculture, education, healthcare, and manufacturing.

These case studies show the value of investing in AI at a regional level, and the importance of global partnerships in driving innovation. As the investment of AI technologies surges, it is essential to ask ourselves: How can we ensure that citizens, cities, and ecosystems benefit from this growth?

How do corporations and venture firms fund these companies and systems? What are the biggest areas where an impact will be felt? It is only with such questions that we can embrace development in artificial intelligence infrastructure.

One way to mobilize an AI-centric transformation is to create a global network of experts and entrepreneurs who can lead the way. This will enable us to exchange knowledge, share resources, and collaborate on projects that have the potential to revolutionize communities around the world. Countries and corporations can leverage public funds and private investments through venture capital firms to boost research, development, and implementation of new AI technologies, particularly in the areas of energy security and sustainability to reshape the environment for the better.

By collaborating and exchanging best practices, humanity can build an interconnected network of AI-driven communities that are capable of working together to resolve complex challenges and create more equitable and sustainable futures for citizens across the globe.

8

AI Culture
and Society

How can social, economic, and ethical criteria be incorporated in research and development to ensure that all segments of society are benefiting? This chapter aims to answer that question.

The social fabric is a complex web of intertwined communities and groups, each with their own needs, interests, and capabilities. Think of it as a quilt that requires everyone's commitment to keep it strong. Artificial intelligence, then, can be seen as an opportunity to link this quilt together and give everyone the same chance of participating in the digital world. The true question is, how can AI be used to bridge the digital divide and ensure fairness in technology? How can AI uphold culture and ensure inclusivity for the human race?

One way to meet these social, economic, and ethical criteria is through research and development that considers the needs of all segments of society. In particular, this includes people with disabilities. According to the World Health Organization, more than a billion people worldwide have some form of disability. It is therefore essential that AI-based developments take into consideration the specific needs of people with disabilities and how AI technologies can help them better sense the world around them. An example would be the use of computer vision to assist those who are blind, or speech recognition and translation technologies for those who are hard of hearing. Imagine AI-based technologies that are designed to help people with limited mobility. This could be done through robotic systems that augment their capabilities and allow them to do things they were otherwise unable to. AI technologies then have the potential to remove many accessibility barriers and create a more equal playing field for all.

While technological advancements can help bridge the digital divide, there are still ethical challenges that need to be considered. These include issues such as inclusivity, bias, privacy, error, expectation setting, simulated data, and social acceptability. For example, black box models and algorithms can have a tendency to exclude certain groups. Therefore, it is important to make sure these models are interpretable, so that any biases or inaccuracies can be identified and corrected before they cause harm. This can be completed through extensive testing and the use of appropriate safeguards, such as transparency and auditing. Transparency refers to the ability to explain how a machine learning model makes decisions, whereas auditing refers to tracking and evaluating the decision-making process.

The challenge, then, is to create an ecosystem in which social justice and equity are upheld. Inclusive AI technologies should be developed in such a way that everyone, regardless of disability or socioeconomic background, can benefit from them. Thankfully, there are four ways to ensure that this happens: by focusing on diversity, transparency, education, and advocacy.

Diversity in the development of AI projects should be a priority. This means recruiting and retaining diverse teams of researchers and engineers to ensure that all perspectives are taken into account and represented. Mark Brayan, CEO of Appen, made his stance clear in a World Economic Forum article: "creating AI that's inclusive requires a full shift in mindset throughout the entirety of the development process."[1] This is important for two reasons: first, it ensures that the AI development reflects the diversity of its users; second, it can help to avoid potential biases and errors.

Next, transparency is key. For any new technology to be successful, it is essential that transparency be embraced in every stage of ideation and design, as well as when selecting the ideal investments and capital. It is critical to make clear what is being created, whom it will benefit most directly, and how it will affect them. For instance, if a certain AI-based system is going to be used to detect crime or fraud, then it should be made clear what data sources and algorithms were used to create the system, as well as how they might impact people in different contexts.

After cultivating an AI built on diversity and transparency, the next step is to educate and provide underrepresented communities with resources that allow them to comprehend—as well as work in—the space of AI. Dr. Brandeis Marshall, founder of DataEdX, Stanford PACS Practitioner Fellow and Partner Research Fellow at Siegel Family Endowment, expressed in a thoughtful discussion that effectively interacting with BIPOC communities representation is essential: "If you don't see it, you won't be it—and that is so vital in order to bring more people into this discipline." This means taking steps to increase the number of people from marginalized communities who have access to education and mentorship in AI. This can be done through collaboration, apprenticeships, and internships with organizations like DataEdX that are dedicated to empowering under-resourced communities to become active participants in the development of responsible data science.

Lastly, advocacy is necessary to guarantee that everyone can benefit from the potential of AI in a safe and equitable way. The public and private sector must support and follow organizations such as Black in AI that have removed barriers faced by people around the world with their programs, along with other great initiatives like Global AI Action Alliance (GAIA). By joining forces, we can raise awareness and make sure that ethical concerns are addressed, as well as create an environment where trust in AI is established.

In order to develop inclusive AI technologies that elevate social justice and equity while also generating successful outcomes, we must focus on diversity, transparency, education, and advocacy. The social fabric is only made richer when everyone is included, and the impact of AI will be greater if those who are often left out are provided with opportunities to contribute to its development. This is why human-centered approaches are needed, to ensure that AI is built with the diverse needs of all people in mind.

Ensuring That Human–Machine Interaction Is "Human-Centered"

"The future is human-centric" is a phrase that is often used when talking about the future of artificial intelligence and machine learning. But what does this even mean? How can we ensure that machines are designed to interact with humans in a way that is beneficial and empowering for both parties?

Let's take a trip down memory lane to when computers first started to become a part of everyday life. Early pioneers of computing in the 1940s had to rely on their technical know-how and specialist knowledge in order to make sense of the new technology. This tech was exclusive to scientists and engineers, with no consideration for the end user. Fast forward to the 1980s, and the concept of "usability" began to be discussed more widely. Early versions of Unix's Ed Editor didn't even have an option to save changes, resulting in users losing their work due to turning off their computers without saving. It was then that the need for user-friendly systems became clear.

Today, the term "human-centered design" is used to describe an approach to engineering and product development that puts people and their context first. The goal of such a design process is to create things that are appropriate for them. This means understanding and solving the root causes of issues rather than just treating symptoms, as well as thinking of the bigger picture and considering the unintended consequences of a product.

The human-aware intelligence (HAI) framework was developed with this in mind, and to ensure that AI solutions are explainable, comprehensible, useful, and usable for people. This framework has three main components: ethically-aligned design, technology that fully reflects human intelligence, and a focus on human factors. Ethically-aligned design is important to ensure that AI solutions avoid discrimination, maintain fairness and justice, and don't replace humans. Technology that fully reflects human intelligence is vital to further enhance AI technology so it can be more like the depth characterized by human intelligence. Human factors design must also be taken into account—for example, user operators must be able to quickly and effectively take over the control of an intelligent system in an emergency.

There are several use cases where the HAI framework can be applied to ensure that human-machine interaction is human-centered. For example, in healthcare applications such as medical imaging and diagnostics, it can help create solutions that are tailored to patient needs while also preserving privacy and autonomy in decision-making. In education, it can be used to create learning systems that are adaptive and personalized, while also encouraging critical thinking. In business, the HAI framework can help to create more user-friendly and effective solutions that are tailored to an organization's specific goals and needs.

Ultimately, human-centered AI design requires a commitment on the part of designers to understand and accommodate human capabilities in order to produce beneficial and empowering results. It also requires an understanding of the technical and ethical implications of AI, as well as the impact it can have on society. By doing this we can ensure that human–machine interactions are truly human-centered—beneficial for both parties and making use of technology to enhance life, not replace it.

Expert Input and Analysis: What Human–Machine Interaction Should Be

By Stephen Ibaraki, Chairman of REDDS Capital, Microsoft 20 Global Awards with 2018–2023 MVP in AI, Investor/Venture Capitalist, Futurist, Founder and Chair of Outreach of UN ITU AI for Good Global Summit

We can ensure that human–machine interaction

- Is human-centered
- Takes into account approaches to social, gender, and economic research
- Avoids bias
- Makes technology transparent and accountable for all communities, so nobody is excluded
- Ensures that our interactions are secure, safe, and private

We do this by taking a transdisciplinary multi-stakeholder process of the more than 300 frameworks, principles, policies, and regulations in the ethics of AI and harmonizing and operationalizing into a universal toolkit and policies to be adhered to by governments, industry, NGOs, academia, civil society, and the UN.

Approaches to Social, Gender, and Economic Research We Should Consider

A new lens on traditional research on social, gender, and economic issues is needed in order to incorporate the new technology of artificial intelligence. AI opens up a range of possibilities for social research, such as improved data processing algorithms and big data analytics. However, with AI also come new challenges in terms of understanding how these developments will affect the way we produce and interpret results.

For instance, AI can help generate more accurate economic models that take into account individual behavior when predicting the impact of policy changes. AI-based microsimulations, such as the AI economist developed by Harvard and Salesforce, incorporate reinforcement learning—a type of AI—in order to simulate economic behavior. This approach has the potential to provide more comprehensive models that better reflect human decisions and responses to public policies.

The Urban-Brookings Tax Policy Center and the Joint Committee on Taxation have long produced microsimulations of tax policy, but these models are limited in their ability to incorporate individual behavioral factors. This limitation is largely due to the difficulty of predicting how individuals will respond to changes in public policy scenarios. However, recent work has suggested that AI may offer a solution.

In particular, AI is well-suited for capturing the nuances of individual behaviors and can provide insights into how people may respond to changing public policy scenarios. For instance, AI models can be used to analyze large data sets containing information about individuals' incomes, spending habits, and other relevant variables that would be difficult to consider in traditional microsimulations.

AI can not only be employed to recognize patterns in individual behaviors that assist in the formation of tax policy decisions, but is also able to uncover new trends and insights that were previously impossible to achieve through conventional research techniques. For instance, AI may reveal unexpected correlations between variables and provide new information that was not previously known or easily accessible. However, it is important to consider that AI tools may also contain bias and errors due to their reliance on existing data sets that could be potentially incomplete or flawed. As such, great care must be taken when using AI in social research and careful steps must be taken to ensure the accuracy of results and insights produced by AI tools.

For the social researcher, AI methods can be applied to facilitate the data collection process. Natural language processing and information extraction algorithms can be used to collect textual data from social media platforms, while computer vision methods such as biometrics, scene understanding, activity recognition, and scene anomaly detection are effective for collecting visual data. Social network analysis is another useful tool for extracting relevant information that may otherwise be hidden or difficult to observe. Finally, behavioral analytics can be used to analyze the behavior of research participants. By harnessing these methods, researchers are able to effectively collect and process data that will provide valuable insights into a wide range of social phenomena.

For example, AI can be used to create virtual learning environments and adapt teaching material for mass open online courses. Similarly, machine translation algorithms can be used in situations where data is presented in different languages, making it easy for researchers to collect information from participants who are located all over the world. All of these techniques allow social researchers to gain access to a wealth of data that would otherwise be inaccessible.

Moreover, a key area within social research is gender studies. AI is being increasingly used to identify gender gaps within data sets and draw conclusions from this analysis. Machine learning algorithms can be applied to detect subtle differences in language usage that are indicative of gender bias or that uncover institutionalized sexism. All of this helps to provide a more nuanced understanding of gender dynamics within social contexts.

The bottom line is that AI provides a powerful tool for social researchers to gain additional insights into the inner workings of society. It is an invaluable source of data and allows us to better understand the complexities of human behavior. As technology progresses, so too will the potential applications of AI in social research, making it an increasingly important part of our research practices. Addressing biases and errors in existing data sets will remain an important priority as we look to harness the numerous benefits of AI and ensure that it is inclusive to all of society.

Avoiding Bias and Making Technology Transparent and Accountable for All Communities

Since the dawn of AI, bias has been one of the main concerns in data-driven technology. Without proper checks and balances, AI can lead to unfair outcomes and discrimination. To ensure responsible AI, transparency is key. We must have an understanding of how algorithms make decisions, what training data sets are used for model development, and what features are excluded from the data set in order to avoid bias. At the same time, we must also build a strong accountability framework that encourages trust and understanding of the technology by all stakeholders—particularly those most impacted by its applications.

First of all, it is important to establish a baseline for responsible data training. To mitigate sample bias and exclusion bias, we need to build large and representative data sets that are free from any preconceived notions or assumptions about relevance or irrelevance of certain features. Further analysis should be done before discarding any feature from the data set, as even seemingly irrelevant features may actually affect the outcome of the model and create an exclusion bias.

In fact, AI has the potential to embed and propagate human biases on a large scale, with worrying consequences. Julia Angwin and ProPublica showed how COMPAS incorrectly labeled African-American defendants as "high-risk" at nearly double the rate of white defendants in Broward County, Florida. Additionally, a tech company had to discontinue development of a hiring algorithm based on analyzing previous decisions when they discovered it penalized applicants from women's colleges. Joy Buolamwini and Timnit Gebru found that facial analysis technologies had higher error rates for certain racial and gender groups—a "CEO image search" returned only 11% female results, despite women making up 27% of US CEOs at the time.[2]

This is why it is essential to have strong checks and balances in place when using AI models. We must ensure that models are not biased toward certain outcomes and that all stakeholders understand the logic of how conclusions are drawn and decisions are made. This means having a clear process for documenting the reasoning behind AI decisions, as well as checks and counterbalances to ensure that the outcomes are fair.

For example, when using AI for employee recruitment or college admissions, it is important to consider broader contextual factors—such as ZIP codes—that may affect the outcome of the model. This helps ensure that decisions are based on merit rather than any preconceived notions or biases. Other checks and balances could include the use of human-in-the loop systems or methods such as explainable AI (XAI) to ensure that models are transparent and understandable.

At first glance, it may appear overwhelming to battle bias and make AI transparent for each community; however, there are three ways to start this process. First, we must audit and examine our data and decision-making systems—including the data sources, algorithms, personas, decisions, and consequences that shape them. We can then create a ledger to measure our technical debt versus technical margin as well as document the logic for how conclusions are drawn (technical debt is the cost of maintaining and updating outdated, inefficient, or obsolete systems, whereas technical margin is the resources and capital available to improve data processes, algorithms, and outcomes). Last, we need to pinpoint the reasoning and logic for why certain decisions were made, as well as provide clear explanations of the consequences of any decision.

Think about it like this: if we don't take the time to understand how AI works and what sort of bias it is prone to, it may perpetuate harmful decisions and outcomes. We must be proactive in building systems that are transparent and accountable—this is the only way we can ensure that technology serves all people equally. With a responsible data training framework in place, we can ensure that AI will be used for the benefit of humanity—rather than against it.

Therefore, I propose the following responsible data techniques to reduce bias in AI models. First, we must eliminate any data or features that could lead to unwanted outcomes or exclusion biases. We should also be careful about the way in which we handle missing or null values—for example, instead of disregarding them, we could impute them with average or median values from the dataset. Additionally, it is important to conduct a proper data audit, which entails understanding the origin of the data and confirming that it is reliable. Finally, we must use a system of checks and balances to ensure that all stakeholders are aware of any decisions made by the AI model and that those decisions are fair and objective.

It's our duty to create equitable and unbiased systems in order to prevent unnecessary suffering and discrimination. This is an urgent issue, but by taking these steps and building a responsible data foundation, we can make sure that AI works for everyone.

Ensuring That Our Interactions Are Safe and Private

In a world where consumer data is a coveted commodity, companies have the responsibility to protect consumers' personal information and ensure that their interactions remain private and secure. To do this, organizations must first understand which data they need in order to serve customers effectively. It is important to collect only the data needed, as well as to revise or write new policies that accommodate different categories of data.

Federated learning is an AI technology that helps to build models on data from different sources without sharing the original information. This is one way businesses can enhance customer privacy while still utilizing the data they need. AI also helps to identify and respond to data breaches more quickly than traditional technologies, as it has no limitations when it comes to monitoring and flagging issues.

It is also important to develop identity and access management practices that are tailored to individuals with roles, as well as security-access levels for different data categories. Further, activity monitoring can help mitigate the risk of insider threats. On top of this, businesses should strive to create an infrastructure environment that is able to accommodate increasing data volumes and technological innovations. On cloud-based platforms, for example, companies should ensure that data is stored in a limited number of systems and that the systems footprint is minimized. Features such as automatic timed logouts and strong password requirements should be built into consumer-facing applications to ensure that security and privacy become default options for consumers. Ultimately, striking a balance between user experience and data protection is key in providing a safe environment for customers.

To better put this in practice, allow me to walk through a potential use case. An e-commerce platform might want to collect information on user behavior, such as browsing history and purchase decisions. AI can be used to analyze this data without collecting identifiable information from the customers themselves. This approach allows for the development of effective models that protect customer privacy while still helping the company build better products and services. Another use case might be a healthcare platform gathering information from patients on their medical history, as well as providing analytics to develop targeted treatments. AI can help here, too, by collecting only the necessary data and keeping user identities anonymous, while still allowing for the development of accurate models that can improve patient outcomes.

At the end of the day, businesses must recognize their responsibility to protect customer data and use the right technologies to ensure that their interactions are safe and private. By taking the necessary steps to build a secure infrastructure, companies can reap the benefits of consumer data while still protecting customer privacy. The key is finding a balance between user experience and data protection—a balance that will ultimately create a safe environment for customers. This is where the General Data Protection Regulation (GDPR) and AI can come together to ensure the best possible outcomes.

AI Privacy: From GDPR to Local and Global Policies

The importance of protecting customer data from misuse and breaches cannot be understated. Consumers are increasingly concerned with how companies use their personal data, and rightfully so. Companies must be vigilant about collecting, using, and storing customer data in an ethical manner, as there are severe consequences for mishandling it.

Fortunately, technology such as AI, security analytics, and encryption can be used to reduce the risk of a data breach. A 2021 report from IBM and the Ponemon Institute revealed that customer personal data (name, email, password) was the most common type of data (44%) exposed in a breach.[3] Utilizing these technologies can help decrease the cost of a breach significantly, saving companies millions of dollars in the process.

Businesses also need to make sure that data is used ethically. A *TechRepublic* report from August 2021 revealed that 78% of consumers are fearful about the amount of data being collected and 40% said they don't trust brands to use their data ethically.[4] Companies should be open and transparent about how customer data is being collected, used, and stored, to build trust with their customers.

In terms of policy and regulation, countries and states are passing consumer data privacy legislation such as the GDPR, the California Consumer Privacy Act (CCPA), and the ePrivacy Directive. These laws are designed to protect customer data from misuse or illicit access. Companies should stay up-to-date on any new policies that may be applicable to their operations in order to remain compliant with the law. This also gives businesses the opportunity to educate consumers on the importance of protecting their own personal data by using strong passwords and two-factor authentication where possible. As a result, a win-win scenario is created, whereby businesses can successfully protect customer data while also gaining the trust of their customers. Trust with customers is very important: a company's reputation is built on the trust of its customers and they are more likely to purchase products and services from a business that they feel has their best interests in mind.

It is therefore in the best interest of companies to take proactive measures to protect customer data with the use of AI, security analytics, and encryption technologies. It's not only smart business, but it's also the right thing to do. The peace of mind that customers will experience will become an invaluable asset as more personal data is shared with businesses in the future.

9 | Social and Financial Inclusion

We are all familiar with the notion of financial and social inclusion—to ensure that people of all backgrounds are seen, heard, and considered in our society. But what does this mean in practice? How do we ensure that everyone has access to the necessary social and financial resources and services to participate fully in our society? To answer these questions, we must deep dive into the very terminology of social and financial inclusion, as well as the policies and programs that create opportunities for all.

First, let's define the term *financial inclusion*. This is used to refer to the idea that everyone should have access to basic financial services, such as bank accounts and credit. In 2020, financial inclusion became more important than ever in light of the global pandemic and its effects on vulnerable populations—especially for those who lost their jobs, or those who had difficulty accessing funds due to lack of banking infrastructure. Financial inclusion became even more important in helping these groups access the necessary resources and services needed in order to survive and thrive.

The United Nations has made financial inclusion an enabler for seven of the 17 Sustainable Development Goals (SDGs), specifically those related to poverty reduction, gender equality, and access to healthcare. The World Bank Group (WBG) is a leading actor in promoting financial inclusion worldwide, with the goal of helping vulnerable populations gain access to transaction accounts that provide key services such as storing money, sending and receiving payments, and facilitating access to other important services. In keeping with this theme, the G20 has outlined its High-Level Principles for Digital Financial Inclusion, which focus on the need to ensure that digital financial services are responsibly delivered and affordable for customers. The significance of these principles is further highlighted by the reality that digital financial services can act as a bridge to not only basic banking needs, but also access to loans, investments, insurance, and other services. Together, these organizations have set up an important framework to promote financial inclusion and ensure that its benefits are accessible to all.

It is also essential to understand the role of social inclusion in achieving financial inclusion. Social inclusion goes beyond financial inclusion—it encompasses the idea that everyone has access not only to money but also to opportunities and resources that allow them to participate fully in their community's life. This includes access to public institutions, employment, housing, health, education, and mobility opportunities. Additionally, it involves recognition of the various forms of marginalization faced by different sectors of society—including issues related to race, gender identity, sexual orientation, or migrant status.

The concept of social inclusion is integral to achieving financial inclusion. Access to basic banking services should not be dependent on a person's social status, regardless of race, gender, or migrant status. In order for financial inclusion to truly benefit all people, it must be accompanied by policies and programs that promote social inclusion as well. But in order for social inclusion to succeed, we must double down on five key tenets: diversity, inequality, digital literacy, inclusion, and ethics.

Diversity can be seen as an essential ingredient for digital innovation. When we include more diverse perspectives in the public discourse, our solutions become more innovative and effective. The latest research has demonstrated that a collective effort of many diverse individuals yields better results than the work of a few experts. And, as technology evolves, it's important to ensure that AI-enabled voice recognition and facial recognition systems don't discriminate against certain genders or skin tones. For example, AI-enabled speech recognition has been documented as struggling with female voices, and facial recognition techniques have trouble identifying darker skin colors.

Inequality is one of the major issues facing digital innovation today. Despite advancements in technology, many people still lack access to basic online services due to financial limitations. According to a Pew Research study, nearly 25% of adults with household incomes below $30,000 don't own a smartphone and over 40% do not have home broadband services or a laptop/desktop computer.[1] And while the majority of adults in higher-income households have access to multiple devices, 13% of those with lower incomes don't have access to any technology at home. To bridge this digital divide, policymakers and businesses must focus on creating initiatives that provide equal access for everyone regardless of their socioeconomic status. For example, digital literacy programs can help people learn how to use technology, thus enabling them to become more competitive in the global economy.

Ariella Lehrer, the CEO of Legacy Games—a gaming company based in the United States—grasps the significance of diversity and inclusion within her industry. Her company focuses on women over 40 years old who enjoy casual gaming. By focusing on this segment, Legacy Games is helping to create an inclusive environment for all ages and genders in order to promote digital literacy in the form of CD-ROMs. As Lehrer explains, "With the move to mobile and streaming, most people don't realize that CD-ROM products are an ongoing business. Our customers still prefer playing puzzle games on PCs for a variety of reasons. Some still do not own a smartphone, and in many parts of the U.S., there continues to be a lack of good internet access. We focus on these customers who are left behind in this transition, although we are trying to bring these customers online."[2] This approach has enabled Legacy Games to continue to serve customers who would otherwise be left behind in the transition to mobile and online gaming.

However, this raises the concern of those who are left out. What kind of exclusion issues could be associated with digital products and services that we may not even think about? In the field of information technology, gender bias is one such issue. Studies have revealed that male applicants are more likely to be hired than female applicants for tech-related jobs, even when the applicants have the same qualifications. Such inequality can have a major impact on the digital landscape, as women may not receive proper recognition and compensation for developing innovative products and services—something that could dampen their motivation to continue innovating.

To combat this, companies must take a proactive stance in promoting diversity and inclusion. Companies can do this by embracing flexible work arrangements for all employees, implementing anti-discrimination policies, and offering ample training opportunities that support career growth. Additionally, organizations must also ensure that they are recruiting from diverse pools of talent to ensure a balanced representation across every level of the company. By promoting a diverse and inclusive work culture, companies can create an environment that allows everyone to thrive—regardless of their gender, race, or other characteristics.

This feeds into the last tenet of social inclusion—ethics. In 2020, the lockdowns and restrictions due to the COVID-19 pandemic shook up our lives and highlighted the importance of ethical principles. Ethical decision-making helps organizations, businesses, and individuals alike make decisions in a manner that is consistent with their values and ultimately leads to better outcomes for all parties involved. Without shared ethical principles, it's difficult to build an equitable and inclusive digital landscape. The easiest way to see this materialize is heavy bias in data sets that can lead to algorithmic inequality.

It's no secret that gender bias has been rampant in medical research. Take heart disease, for example: traditionally seen as a male affliction, it has led to countless women being misdiagnosed or completely ignored when it comes to treatment and diagnosis. This is just one instance of how excluding female test subjects can have serious, long-lasting implications in the field of healthcare. To truly understand and tackle such health issues, it's essential to include both genders in research studies so that we can have a more holistic view of the human body.

Another example is Amazon's former AI hiring system. The company had to terminate its AI hiring system because of an observed gender bias. After analyzing resumes from many job applications submitted over the prior decade, the algorithm was designed in a manner that favored male candidates and limited features related to women. This sort of technology can have major repercussions if these biases are not rectified.

These examples demonstrate how having a shared set of ethical principles helps create an equitable and inclusive digital landscape. By having a clear understanding of what is right or wrong, organizations can make sure they do not perpetuate the cycle of bias and inequality. Making ethical decisions goes a long way in promoting social inclusion and creating a digital environment that can be enjoyed by everyone.

Both the public and private sectors have roles to play in social and financial inclusion. For one, governments should ensure that citizens have access to the digital infrastructure and services they need, while also creating policies and regulations that protect consumer rights. Meanwhile, businesses should prioritize creating a safe and secure environment for their employees, customers, and other stakeholders. Action items such as these can help us create a digital landscape that includes everyone and allows them to fully participate in the digital economy.

Social Impact at the Enterprise Level

Social enterprise—using business to create social change—is becoming increasingly popular as a means of tackling difficult global challenges. Artificial intelligence AI has become an integral tool in the arsenal of many organizations, allowing companies to identify opportunities for improvement and make more informed decisions that consider the impact on society.

Take autonomous and connected vehicles (AVs and CVs) as an example. These technologies are being used to reduce traffic congestion, energy consumption, and environmental impact while at the same time providing efficient transportation alternatives for those who may not have access to traditional modes of transport. Whereas traditional methods of transportation may require numerous returns to the same location, AI-driven AVs and CVs can optimize travel times and reduce emissions by using "smart" systems that learn from past trips. Similarly, distributed energy grids, managed by AI, can optimize the use of energy resources, leading to lower overall utility bills and improved public health outcomes. For instance, AI-driven systems can identify energy waste, suggest energy efficient alternatives, and provide real-time feedback to optimize the use of resources.

One of the key ways in which these efficiencies have been achieved is through the development of smart cities. Smart cities involve a combination of AI, robotics, and connected technology that strengthen the urban infrastructure by creating more efficient living spaces. Some of the world's top smart cities include Singapore's Smart Nation program and the Kingdom of Saudi Arabia's NEOM project. The Smart Nation project has enabled Singapore to reduce its energy consumption and CO_2 emissions through the use of AI-powered solutions such as autonomous vehicles, smart meters, and intelligent street lighting. Similarly, NEOM has used AI-driven technologies such as facial recognition and voice analytics to create a "smart city" that is seamlessly connected, enabling residents to access real-time data such as traffic updates and emergency services.

AI can also have positive social impacts at the enterprise level, helping to optimize operations while minimizing negative environmental impacts. OYAK Cimento, a Turkish cement manufacturing group, is using AI to significantly reduce their carbon footprint by increasing operational efficiency with lower unit energy consumption. If the company were to produce 1 million tons of cement per year, just a 1% reduction in clinker production is estimated to result in the absorption of 320,000 trees of CO_2 per year.

All of this contributes to another essential component of enterprise-level social change, which is the issue of climate change. Artificial intelligence can be a potent force in the battle against climate change. Autonomous vehicles, for example, may diminish our emissions by 50% over the next three decades due to their ability to compute and execute the most fuel-efficient routes. Additionally, AI has had remarkable effects on agriculture—peanut farmers in India have seen an astonishing 30% improvement in harvests since using AI technology.

Smart agriculture and smart disaster response are two examples of how AI can be used to create social and environmental impact. Smart agriculture involves the use of intelligent systems to optimize crop yields, reduce water and fertilizer waste, and improve pest management. Similarly, AI-driven systems can help emergency response teams make more informed decisions during natural disasters by providing real-time monitoring of weather conditions, storm paths, power outages, and other important data. Moreover, climate informatics is an AI-driven field that uses machine learning to analyze data related to climate change. This data can be used to identify potential risks associated with climate change, such as rises in sea level or extreme weather events.

AI-powered systems have the potential to transform how we measure and manage our carbon footprint, helping us meet new regulations while reducing our environmental impact. In a 2020 study focusing on AI's potential role in achieving the UN's 17 Sustainable Development Goals, which encompass social, economic, and environmental objectives, researchers found that AI could positively enable 93% of the environmental targets. These include the building of smart and low-carbon cities, integrating renewable energy sources through smart grids, using IoT devices to monitor electricity consumption, detecting desertification trends via satellite imagery, and tackling marine pollution.

The use cases for AI-powered social change are nearly endless. By coupling AI with human ingenuity, we can create a global society that is far more connected and sustainable than ever before. In this way AI is a true source of empowerment for future industries, economies, and communities.

Empowering Future Industries with AI

The *Jetsons* cartoon of the 1960s depicted a world in which robots played an integral role in day-to-day life. While the Jetsons' world may have seemed far-fetched at the time, today's reality looks increasingly similar to it. AI has become an important force across multiple industries, and its impact is only growing with each passing day.

A perfect example of the power of AI is in the automotive industry, which has seen a dramatic shift in recent years. Automakers have been investing heavily in connected services and ride-sharing platforms, making use of self-driving car technology to revolutionize transportation. With the involvement of tech companies, traditional industry boundaries are crumbling and ushering in a new era of mobility. The Indian Railways have taken precautionary measures to guarantee that meals are served in clean and healthy conditions by teaming up with the Delhi-based startup WOBOT. To ensure hygiene compliance, high-definition CCTV cameras were installed to monitor food preparation live. This AI-powered system detects not only rodent activity but also other sanitation concerns—all of which can be remedied swiftly, ensuring that an elevated level of health standards is met at all times.

AI has also been making waves in healthcare, with the emergence of wearables and pharma companies providing rich data insights. The use of on-body sensors, home behavior sensors, and real-time diagnostic services is becoming increasingly popular among medical professionals. The Tamil Nadu e-Governance Agency (TNeGA) has pioneered an AI-based mobile app to detect cataracts, thereby eliminating preventable blindness in the state. This ambitious endeavor seeks to address the absence of resources for detecting this condition and aims to improve lives through technology.

The power of AI is being felt across industries, with farming, manufacturing, and banking industries also taking advantage of it. Farming has seen a shift away from traditional operations as AI-powered systems have been able to improve crop yields and reduce costs. As an example, ICRISAT developed a sowing app driven by AI to accurately predict when local farmers should sow their seeds. As a result of this innovation, harvests have risen 10–30%. Moreover, the use of AI technology can be leveraged to join forces with rural financial institutions and grant farmers access to much-needed capital resources. In manufacturing, researchers at IIT Kharagpur have developed an innovative and cost-effective Industry 4.0 approach for real-time metrological analysis utilizing AI. This technique can be used to objectively assess every job in a batch quickly, accurately, and economically. Furthermore, the AI-enabled system is capable of enhancing the image quality taken from low-cost cameras to a level similar to high-quality cameras and can process the image swiftly. It also automates the acceptance or denial of production operations, providing instantaneous feedback to managers.

The banking sector has been drastically improved by the introduction of AI-based frameworks, such as HDFC's EVA (electronic virtual assistant). Since it was first introduced, this technology has served over 3 million customers smoothly. From detecting credit card fraud to providing customer support and analyzing market trends, these tasks have become simpler with the help of the groundbreaking AI software in place.

The entertainment industry has also started to leverage AI for content curation and recommendation. The online streaming giant Netflix has successfully implemented a proprietary algorithm that allows it to customize the library of available titles according to user preferences.

All of this goes to show that AI is changing the way businesses operate and creating a world of endless possibilities. AI technologies have already made an impact in many industries, and they're likely to continue doing so as more companies embrace AI's potential for innovation. With so much power at their fingertips, AI will help organizations create smarter products and services, reach new markets, enhance customer experiences, and make better decisions. This feeds directly into the core theme of this book—social impact and the elevation of human capacity. AI technologies are helping to bridge the gap between communities and enhance global knowledge, while also enabling people to lead more productive and meaningful lives.

GPT and Business Strategy

When it comes to generative AI, particularly ChatGPT, there is a lot of excitement and discussion around it, from celebrities to the rest of us. However, for serious businesses, it's important to focus on the strategic implications of generative AI and AI in general. This means understanding how it will change the organization's direction and functionality, not just relying on data scientists.

While ChatGPT is a step forward for open AI, there are still gaps to be filled, such as explainable AI, which remains a crucial missing piece in the puzzle. It's important for businesses to carefully consider the impact of generative AI and incorporate it into their overall strategy for success.

In order to effectively implement AI across various industries, it is crucial to have a well-planned strategy in place. Generative AI has the potential to impact a multitude of areas such as marketing, customer service, and engineering, but it is essential to consider how this technology will impact the organization as a whole. Rapid action is necessary as the pace of technological advancement continues to accelerate.

Furthermore, it is important for businesses to understand their current business model and how it can be adapted to incorporate generative AI. This technology goes beyond simple data searches and can greatly transform the way a business operates. Therefore, careful consideration and planning must be undertaken to fully realize its potential benefits.

Time is of the essence, as the pace of technological advancement continues to accelerate. In particular, businesses must consider how generative AI will impact industries such as law and healthcare, including potential changes to diagnostic processes and the preservation of private information. Creating new business models and leveraging generative AI as a competitive edge will be necessary for success in this rapidly evolving landscape.

It is imperative to have a comprehensive plan in place to mitigate risks associated with generative AI. As we delve deeper into generative AI and analyze data, we must be mindful of misinformation and fake information that can arise. This brings up pertinent questions about data ownership, bias, and copyright protection. It is crucial to establish a risk strategy that includes ethical AI, bias and fake recognition, threat security, talent training, and creativity enhancement.

Before rolling out generative AI, we must address these complex risks and develop solutions to counter them. It is important to ensure that generative AI doesn't just take care of basic and remedial tasks but also helps humans to focus on more creative tasks at hand. Therefore, it is imperative to have a well-crafted plan in place to manage the risks associated with generative AI.

Social Impact Created by Enterprises

From climate to economic development, the impact of corporations in the context of social responsibility has become increasingly important. Corporations are facing heightened scrutiny, with stakeholders demanding greater accountability and transparency in their practices. Consequently, it is essential to investigate the intricacies of topics that shape social progress such as climate change, health and well-being, enhanced infrastructure and mobility solutions, public involvement in affairs of state, energy conservation strategies, and AI/XR (extended reality) applications for city living.

It is widely acknowledged that companies have a responsibility to reduce their environmental footprints. A 2017 Carbon Majors report found that just 100 companies are responsible for 71% of global emissions.[3] Initiatives such as the Paris Agreement and the UN Sustainable Development Goals have put pressure on corporations to reduce their carbon footprints, but evidence suggests that many companies still lag behind when it comes to climate action.

The advent of AI has created yet another challenge for businesses in terms of minimizing emissions. AI-powered supercomputers are powered by the public electricity grid and supported by backup diesel-powered generators, meaning that a single AI system can emit over 250,000 pounds of carbon dioxide. In Chile, the second-largest producer of lithium in the world, lithium mines are so water-intensive that they consume 65% of the region's water. This has caused native species of flora and fauna to become endangered and affected local populations.

The need for sustainability initiatives is becoming more paramount than ever, especially in light of the climate crisis. Corporations need to develop strategies that incorporate the use of AI and XR applications, but with an eye toward sustainability. Companies must be mindful of their surroundings when implementing new technologies, addressing potential damage to land and ecosystems caused by construction or extraction projects. Innovative solutions such as renewable energy sources and carbon offsets could help minimize emissions generated by data farms. Moreover, corporations should consider the impact of AI on local communities, ensuring that they are consulted and their rights respected. This ties directly into the next key discussion topic—health and well-being—as it is often communities on the front lines of climate change that are most affected by environmental degradation.

The adage "an ounce of prevention is worth a pound of cure" is particularly applicable when considering the social impact of businesses. In order to create positive, lasting effects on society and their stakeholders, organizations need to be proactive about implementing interventions that protect people's health and well-being. Research has shown that, with the right strategies in place, businesses can have a positive and long-term impact on society.

For instance, businesses can use AI to help identify patterns that could lead to potential health risks or depression in their employees or customers. AI also has the potential to improve productivity and efficiency of care delivery, enabling healthcare systems to provide more and better care to more people. Furthermore, AI-generated maps such as those developed by Massachusetts General Hospital may be used to guide individuals toward improved mental well-being. Such initiatives can also be used to identify and intervene in depression-prone psychological configurations, contributing to a healthier society.

Businesses should also take into account the importance of social capital valuation when assessing and managing their social impact. Social capital is created when businesses invest in the people, communities, and environment around them. By measuring the impact of social capital, businesses can better understand and track their long-term impacts on society. For example, investments in education and training may lead to increased opportunities for local employment, while efforts to improve air quality through green initiatives can contribute to enhanced well-being.

Green initiatives are not just limited to environmental sustainability, but can also encompass the well-being of a business's workforce. Companies should take into account mental health and well-being in the workplace and implement policies that promote healthy working environments such as flexible working hours, independent work opportunities, and professional development programs. Furthermore, initiatives such as providing mindfulness or meditation classes may help employees to better manage stress and anxiety, leading to increased productivity. AI can be leveraged to enhance such programs, providing personalized interventions for employees in need.

By taking a holistic approach to social impact management, businesses can ensure that their investments are yielding tangible outcomes for stakeholders and society as a whole. With the right strategies in place, organizations can have a direct, positive effect on the well-being of their employees and customers as well as on their communities and the environment. By taking a proactive approach to social impact management, businesses can create lasting positive effects on society.

Infrastructure is a lasting social impact investment that can improve access to services and resources, such as education and healthcare. Companies have begun investing in digitizing their infrastructure, with launches of government portals creating a more efficient system. For instance, Indian Prime Minister Narendra Modi launched the MyGov website in 2014, which utilized an AI-enabled chatbot for communication during the COVID-19 pandemic.[7] But it's not just digital infrastructure that can bring about social change.

Natural calamities, such as floods, can also have a major impact on society. Companies are investing in AI-based flood prediction models to provide 48-hour warnings to people living in vulnerable areas, giving them more time to prepare and safeguard their lives and livelihoods. For example, the flood prediction model was first launched in India's Bihar and is now being extended across the country, with multilingual messages tailored to individual areas through infographics and maps.

Education is also an important social impact investment for businesses, as it can open up new opportunities for children from underprivileged backgrounds. According to the Central Board of Secondary Education (CBSE) in India, AI has been incorporated into the school curriculum to ensure that students get the fundamental information and skills of computer science, mechanical learning, and artificial intelligence. The Ministry of Electronics and Information Technology (MeitY) has also launched the "Responsible AI for Youth" program in April 2014, which saw more than 11,000 government school students complete basic courses in AI.

The key takeaways here are that a sustainable social impact investment doesn't just revolve around financial donations. By investing in things like digital infrastructure, natural disaster prediction models, and educational programs, companies can help create lasting change that will bring tangible benefits to society as a whole.

And infrastructure isn't only the brick and mortar of roads and bridges—it's what empowers people to move through and access their community, to build it up and participate in it. The advancement of technology has allowed for increased opportunities for individuals to become more mobile. Social impact enterprises have had a hand in driving this change, as they are committed to providing resources and tools that can dramatically improve the mobility of people living with disabilities or those who might not otherwise have access to enhanced transportation options.

For instance, artificial intelligence has been a major driving force in creating solutions that allow those with visual impairments to more easily access mail, read documents, and otherwise navigate the world. Voice-activated virtual assistants such as Amazon Alexa or Google Home can be used by people with reduced mobility to control appliances and access information. Other examples include Seeing AI—an app that translates words into audio for visually impaired individuals so they can stay connected without requiring assistance from others—as well as IFTTT, an app that automates tasks to help those with poor dexterity access their smartphone's functionalities.

Moreover, AI has enabled enterprises to create innovative solutions that allow individuals to move with greater freedom and safety. In addition, AI-powered solutions can reduce travel costs and optimize the use of transport infrastructure. For example, ride-sharing services such as Uber or Lyft use AI algorithms for route optimization and dynamic pricing of rides. This helps to reduce congestion on roads and enables individuals to use the service even in places where public transport is not available.

Mobility is ultimately a key factor in ensuring social inclusion. Without an inclusive approach to mobility, certain members of society are left behind. For this reason, it is essential for businesses to equip citizens with the means and materials they require to participate in society.

By providing individuals with the means to move freely and independently, businesses are taking a step toward promoting social inclusion. This is becoming increasingly important in today's digital age, as companies understand that social responsibility goes beyond charity and volunteering. Indeed, giving back to the community is an integral part of a business model's sustainability, and the social license to operate (SLO) is gaining prominence as an essential factor for a company's successful operation.

SLO refers to the public acceptance of a company's right to exist and operate, but it must be earned through engagement and collaboration with all stakeholders. This means that companies should involve their social actors in decision-making through multi-stakeholder partnerships, while being mindful of the potential impacts on society. Moreover, companies should take into account the digital inequalities that might be generated by their operations and use their technological advances to narrow the existing gaps in society.

Additionally, enterprises must understand that if they just focus on economic gains, this will eventually result in public backlash when individuals lose trust in them. Ethical behavior must become part of a company's corporate culture and decision-making process. To that end, companies should be more transparent when it comes to their operations, publicly articulate their social responsibilities, implement appropriate governance structures, and open up communication channels with stakeholders in order to engage in meaningful dialogue that will shape the public's perception of them.

Through SLO, businesses can create a higher level of trust with the public, build better relationships, and achieve long-term success by contributing to society. It is a win-win situation, as companies have the opportunity to use innovative technologies while adapting their operations in order to generate positive social impact and advance sustainability. Consequently, SLO should be embraced by all enterprises as it provides an effective way to balance economic prosperity and social responsibility in today's digital era.

The ultimate question is: How can we use SLO to advance the public interest while creating sustainable business models? This requires all stakeholders—companies, governments, and communities—to come together and create a collective responsibility for sustainability. It is only through collaboration that the collective effort to reach the SLO goals can be successful. It is for that reason that multi-stakeholder partnerships and dialogues need to be established in order to create a mutually beneficial relationship between stakeholders, reduce conflicts, and generate positive outcomes for all parties involved.

In addition to multi-stakeholder partnerships, artificial intelligence and data analysis can provide an additional layer of coordination necessary for a successful energy transition. A shift to a more sustainable, low-carbon system is essential for long-term global well-being. To accomplish this transformation successfully, we need an intelligent coordination layer that can help stakeholders identify patterns and insights in data, learn from experience, and model possible outcomes of complex situations.

The energy industry is at the heart of both economic and social progress. A shift to a more sustainable, low-carbon system is essential for long-term global well-being. To accomplish this transformation successfully, we need an intelligent coordination layer that can help stakeholders identify patterns and insights in data, learn from experience, and model possible outcomes of complex situations.

But complexity is the key challenge. Decarbonizing energy systems requires coordination across the entire value chain, from production to consumption, and presents a huge challenge from both a technological and an economic perspective. AI can be used to bridge this gap by providing decision-makers with meaningful insights into energy system performance.

The application of AI in the energy industry has already demonstrated its potential to improve renewable energy forecasting, grid operations, coordination of distributed assets, and demand-side management. AI can provide accurate forecasts on the amount of renewables available at any given moment, enabling power grid operators to make smarter decisions about when and how to optimally leverage renewable energy sources.

For example, AI-driven technologies can provide accurate predictions of solar, wind, and hydroelectric output. By using these forecasts, grid operators can more effectively manage their electricity supply systems—allowing them to achieve greater efficiencies and reduce costs associated with energy production and distribution. Additionally, AI can help optimize the network of distributed resources within a system by making it easier to identify and store excess energy when needed.

AI can also be used to create more intelligent demand-side management systems, which allow for greater efficiency in the use of energy resources by automatically adjusting consumption patterns according to user needs. This could open up unprecedented opportunities for new business models, from peer-to-peer energy trading to home automation services.

Finally, AI could be used to develop more efficient materials and processes for a zero-emissions energy system. For example, AI can identify the most effective components and production methods for certain types of batteries or solar panels—leading to lower-cost renewable energy sources.

This bleeds into the discussion of urban life experiences and energy efficiency, which AI can support by helping cities and communities optimize their energy usage to reduce impacts on the environment.

Experiences are the driving force for developments in urban environments. In the past, these experiences have centered around physical space—the streets and buildings of cities. But with advances in artificial intelligence (AI) and extended reality (XR), urban life experiences are now being freed from physical limitations.

From virtual museums to virtual retail stores, AI and XR are revolutionizing how people experience cities. AI is enabling cities to provide a more personalized experience that changes in real time based on user preferences and city conditions. XR further enhances these experiences by creating immersive digital environments that are not constrained by physical boundaries. Together, AI and XR make it possible for people to explore the world around them with unprecedented depth and detail.

The potential for enterprises to use AI and XR for social impact is vast. These technologies can be applied to a range of problems, from improving access to public services and providing better city navigation tools to helping people connect with their local communities. They can also be used in more creative ways, such as creating virtual museums, educational experiences, and other forms of digital entertainment.

For example, AI and XR can be used to create interactive, immersive experiences in public spaces. This could mean giving busy urban dwellers a chance to take a break by participating in a virtual art exhibition or exploring an augmented reality garden. It could also include developing applications that allow people to virtually explore their local communities, discover new restaurants and shops, or even get recommendations from local experts.

The possibilities for AI and XR to create meaningful social impact are immense. By leveraging the power of these technologies, businesses can provide unique experiences that enhance urban life, while providing real-world benefits to those living in the city. These technologies can be used to improve accessibility for disabled individuals, provide vital services such as healthcare in remote areas, and even reduce crime rates by providing more accurate analysis of suspicious activity. It is also possible that these technologies can help bridge the gap between different social classes, by providing access to educational opportunities and other amenities in underserved areas.

Building on this, enterprises should focus on creating solutions that bring real-world benefits to the people who live and work in cities. This could include providing interactive experiences that teach people about important topics, such as reducing energy consumption or exploring the latest innovations in urban infrastructure. It could also involve developing applications that help people connect with others, learn new skills, and find jobs.

As AI and XR become increasingly ubiquitous, businesses should strive to not only maximize the potential of these technologies for their own profit, but also use them to foster positive social impact. By leveraging the power of AI and XR, enterprises can create experiences that revolutionize how people interact with urban life. This could be a key step in creating a more equitable and enjoyable future for all.

PART IV

Foreseeing the Future

As with all advances of humankind, the youth are the key to the future. In this section I discuss how the youth of today work to build the world of tomorrow. The future is bright, and I can see its potential in my own home, with my amazing daughter.

10 | Future Cities and Societies

Let's take all of these parts and build the future. For the rest of this book I want you to let go of the constraints you currently have in your mind as to what is possible, and imagine what can be. If you were to be able to tell a person in 1890 what the world looks like today, and how we got here, they couldn't even wrap their mind around it. We can begin building a future you can't imagine, starting now.

Technology changes everything, and how we design our cities needs to be rooted in the most advanced AI available. AI will drive the most effective, efficient, and people-first cities ever to exist on Earth. From basic infrastructure of sewers, water supply, electric grids, roads, parks, fire and police stations, and schools, we can leverage the power of AI to design cities that work for everyone. The change has begun, and is projected to continue to expand, with global revenue for smart city technologies, products, and services projected to reach an estimated $241 billion in 2023.[1]

Reshaping Ecosystems and Urban Design with AI

Urban designers and planners now have the ability to use AI to lay out an entirely new urban area, or improve on existing ones. In so doing, we will see cities that were created with a strategy based on real-time data. These will be sustainable strategies that adjust as data is ingested. AI will then aid urban planners in their decisions on traffic routes (for public and private transportation), bettering the flow of the entire city while lessening commute times for citizens, and increasing efficiency of waste pickup and delivery of goods. The city will be responsive to its citizens instead of citizens having to constantly modify their lives to navigate their city.

Reshaping Public Health

The World Health Organization reports that between 3 and 8 million people die prematurely every year, due to the air they are breathing being contaminated with harmful pollutants that negatively affect their respiratory systems. AI can be used to detect and report in real time when air quality is poor and notify authorities and residents. Such devices are already in use in places like Germany, the United States, Lima, and Africa. As we have talked through earlier in this book, this data will not exist in isolation. If a city is truly a smart city, this data will talk to all other inputs and track everything that is happening that day, week, and month to extrapolate correlations as to the cause, and then work to create solutions or ways to mitigate pollution creation.

My home base is New York, and in my travels for work I visit Japan, Miami, and cities in the Middle East and around Europe, and one thing every city has in common is the massive amount of waste produced. Imagine for one second if trash removal and waste management simply stopped working for two weeks. The cities would be unlivable, deadly even. AI can be implemented to lessen the amount of labor needed to clean our cities, make waste management and removal more efficient, and ensure that recycling is being used to its maximum potential.

London-based Greyparrot developed a tool that identifies and sorts different types of waste, reducing the labor and time needed while increasing the accuracy of recycling. Inventions like Bin-e can lead to 92% accuracy in recycling sorting by using an AI-based recognition system.[2] This technology needs to be scaled for entire urban areas. Instead of trash trucks arbitrarily going street to street based on the day of the week, we need an AI map and schedule created to tell our drivers which bins to collect each day in the most efficient manner possible. This will eliminate unnecessary stops and inform data as to which areas and specific businesses create the most waste.

Reshaping Public Safety

AI is currently being used across the globe in several ways that increase public safety and, in turn, increase public health:

- Preventive policing
- Combating terrorist threats
- Responding to natural disasters
- Crowd and traffic control
- Mitigating and responding to emergencies

As more and more municipalities increase their use and leverage of AI, we will see an uptick in public safety and health.

Creating Smart Cities

Evolution has been slow but steady, in the right direction. Starting with something as seemingly simple as synchronization of traffic lights, moving to technologies such as the IoT, AI and cloud services are being used today to make our cities smart and work better.

There next needs to be a true merger between leaders of cities and their citizens to become co-creators of their worlds. The input of citizens is crucial for city planners to get as granular as possible into what matters to the people they are planning the city for. What are their current pain points, what do they wish existed, what do they want to see done away with? No, not all requests can be met, but the data is needed and will be informative to design and future planning.

The harmony of people and AI again comes to the center. We, the people, have the key to driving innovation, not for innovation's sake, but for the betterment of our immediate world.

Creating Cognitive Cities

Microsoft's Redmond headquarters are smart and connected. The campus is comprised of 125 buildings creating 2,000,000 pieces of data registering 500,000,000 transactions every 24 hours. Complete digitalization was required for the campus to become a single asset. This reduces waste and improves building efficiency. Through the use of AI they experience energy savings of 6–10%, are able to handle over 10,000 requests per month for technical assistance, and correct 48% of problems in just 60 seconds—all of that and producing an ROI in a year and a half.

How We Connect Energy, Water, Environment, and Climate Efficiency

As I have written throughout this book, no one piece of technology, or use of AI, can exist independent of others. Everything must talk and work together. This is no different when building smart cities. Traffic systems must work in concert with waste management, which must work with power, natural gas, and electric grids. The police, fire, and public health and safety departments must be able to read and interpret this data, while simultaneously inputting data into the same AI information hub.

This all must be leveraged to better distribute natural resources within a smart city to improve the overall climate, air, water, and so on of the city for its inhabitants. Smart AI-driven environment technologies that are installed in cities using all the data points just mentioned result in hyperaccurate urban data, creating highly productive interventions, enabling cities to use their resources sustainably.[3]

Not only are these cities smart, they are sustainable in every way imaginable. This is the future we must plan and fight for. Numbers from the World Bank show that 56% of the world's population (4.4 billion) live in cities today, and by 2050 an estimated 7 of 10 people will live in cities.[4] With current technology, the examples from across the globe, and the game plan created by Microsoft it is imperative that as a human society we move at a hastened pace toward global implementation of smart cities.

Creating Tomorrow's AI-Driven Communities

We can observe cities such as Dublin and Singapore embracing the use of digital twins—a dynamic digital representation of their physical assets and environments and their interdependencies—for urban planning. Through the use of machine learning, these replicas can predict future events or trends. This technology can be used to provide assistance with everyday operations, simulate a natural disaster's potential effect on the city, or assess wind flow in order to guarantee shade in parks and streets. With advanced technology that provides faster root-cause analysis identification, digital twins will become increasingly powerful for data-driven decision-making and will be adopted by many city governments as a means of increasing resiliency.[5] ABI research predicts that by 2025 there will be more than 500 digital twins, while ESI ThoughtLab predicts that investments in this technology from cities will rise from 11% in 2021 to 31% by 2026—an increase of almost 300%.[6]

11 | The Next Generation

This chapter covers how youth can use AI to have a positive impact on all people.

The Global Shapers Community works to reduce inequalities worldwide by empowering youth to take action. It provides them with a platform to build their own responsible AI initiatives, whether technical or policy and governance-related, so that they can have an equal voice in any given AI ecosystem and can influence the trajectory of the technology. For example, the Stanford-incubated AI4ALL[1] program targeted high school students and produced projects to examine inequalities, improve the criminal justice system, improve patient outcomes, and provide feedback to surgeons through computer vision. Intel's AI for Youth also created projects focusing on cyber-bullying, energy efficiency, and educational support. By uniting youth from several continents in multilateral convenings such as the United Nations Framework Convention on Climate Change (UNFCCC) did in 2009 with the intergovernmental climate change convenings, we ensure that their voices are heard and their stakeholder status is secured.

As another example, at the U&AI Camp, an international youth bootcamp, more than 1,300 young people from more than 50 countries across Eurasia, America, Africa, and Oceana presented their innovative AI solutions for advancing the Sustainable Development Goals (SDGs).[2] The winning team, WeReco, designed an e-commerce mobile app platform that directs users to eco-friendly products. The runner-up was Aket, which proposed a WeChat mini app to link suppliers with food near its expiration date with individual consumers. In third place was AI Care with a proposal to improve elderly health through long-term behavior monitoring using computer vision.

In Bangalore, India, 10th-grader Rahul Jaikrishna developed Cyber Detective—an artificial intelligence-based model with an accuracy of up to 80% that detects cyberbullying—after he learned that "confession pages" created by school students—online diaries on social media where young people post confessions and secrets—often make teens easy targets for bullying.

Four 17-year old Polish students[3]—Jakub Florkowski, Antoni Marcinek, Wiktoria Gradecka, and Wojciech Janicki—from Jan Kanty High School used their skills from Intel AI for Youth to create the Hey Teacher! app. The app helps interested students in Poland easily locate competent teaching resources to strengthen or broaden their knowledge via private tutoring by matching them with private tutors through filters such as subject, level of education, availability, location, and price. June 2019 saw four students at Busan Computer High School in South Korea notice a large amount of energy being wasted when they entered an empty computer lab. Despite not being in use, the lab's air-conditioning, lights, and PCs were still on. To address this issue, Lee Jihong, Kim Eundong, Kim Jidong, and Lee Seungyun created Energy Guard—an AI algorithm that pairs a PC and a webcam with computer vision and other analytics to count the number of people present in a room and toggle on or off the room's power supply accordingly. The system is currently in pilot at the school's PC lab with plans to expand it to over 30 rooms in the school with a goal of covering over 10,000 classrooms across South Korea.

Roadmap for the Future

In order to prepare for a sustainable AI future, it is essential that we create a framework and roadmap for society. This requires a collective effort from future-thinking enterprises, individuals, and policymakers to address the social impact of AI and prevent any negative consequences. It is important to measure both the positive and negative effects of AI and work toward a human-centric approach to ensure a sustainable future for the planet.

Expert Input and Analysis: What Young People Are Saying

By Toshie Takahashi, AI for Good; Youth and AI/Robots; Professor of Waseda University, Tokyo; Associate Fellow of the CFI at the University of Cambridge

According to the "a future with AI" project, in collaboration with the United Nations, young people suggested that the following eight statements must be considered to create a sustainable AI society, in a global context:

AI is part of our future.

We need to find a successful and happy coexistence of humans and AI.

Collaboration between AI and humans is a powerful combination.

AI carries serious risks, but they can be controlled.

Important areas where AI can help are equality and the environment.

AI should never be allowed to autonomously kill people.

There should be international rules on the design of AI by scientists and engineers.

There should be international rules on the use of AI by companies or governments.

We can see some tensions between opportunities and risks among the above statements; however, the most important thing is that young generations believe that humans have the capability to overcome the new risks associated with AI.

In order to maximize new opportunities and minimize risks, we must consider, discuss, and learn "smart wisdom" in the age of AI. Smart wisdom emerges as people reflexively create and recreate themselves as they make sense of life and their place in an AI society while appropriating the power and possibilities offered by new technological innovation.

(continued)

> Governments and industries should provide AI education as well as career advice and support to young people to prepare them for a world with AI. If they reflexively create and recreate themselves and their AI communities with smart wisdom, a human-first AI society could emerge.

Recent events have highlighted the potential dangers of AI, with concerns about its impact on financial, economic, security, and human core values. The president of the United States, Joe Biden, has publicly acknowledged the risks of AI and the need for action. As we continue to witness the disruptive power of new AI technologies like ChatGPT, it is crucial that regulators and lawmakers take necessary steps to mitigate potential harms and promote ethical and responsible AI development. We need to provide a framework for addressing these complex issues and fostering a sustainable future for all.

From a broader perspective, it is evident that artificial intelligence is significantly transforming companies and enterprises, and how we live. The integration of personal assistants such as Siri, Alexa, and Google into our daily lives, as well as the development of new autonomous vehicles, are just a few examples of the impact of AI. However, in order for AI solutions to be fully integrated into company systems, we must address issues of transparency and data security.

AI Regulation Efforts

Efforts to regulate AI are gaining momentum in the United States, led by Senator Chuck Schumer, who aims to introduce legislation to regulate AI. While Europe has already proposed various strategic documents and frameworks for the regulation of AI, it is essential to develop a human-centric and sustainable AI future that measures both positive and negative social impacts. Through developing a framework and roadmap, individuals, enterprises, and regulators can work together to mitigate the risks and potential negative impacts of AI while maximizing the benefits it offers.

It is imperative to establish a comprehensive framework and roadmap toward a sustainable, human-centric future for AI on the planet. Enterprises and individuals alike must prepare for this future and agree on its direction, while measuring its social impact and minimizing negative effects. Recent events, including concerns from regulators, lawmakers, and citizens regarding the financial, economic, security, social, and human core values impact of AI have prompted efforts to legislate and regulate AI at the congressional level in the United States and at the Union Commission level in Europe.

Additionally, we must address bias and fairness in training data sets, as they can have detrimental effects on different ethnic groups, geographic areas, and age groups. Responsible implementation of AI technologies must remove biases, ensure fairness, and provide transparency with explainability. This is particularly crucial with the emergence of powerful language models like ChatGPT, which contain massive amounts of information and data. Enterprises must adopt a responsible approach toward delivering information and implementing emerging technologies in a way that incorporates these considerations into a new framework.

Society 5.0

Japan is exploring a new model called Society 5.0, which centers around placing humans at the forefront of societal changes. This was announced by the Japanese government during their G20 meeting in 2019, and it is an interesting new approach, with robotics and advancements being driven by humans. The outdated models of Industry 4.0, which simply focus on optimization and efficiency, are no longer relevant. The key factors for our new future are human-centricity, sustainability, and resilience. Projects like Europe Fit for the Digital Age are seriously discussing this topic.

It is crucial to build a framework with prerequisites that focus on higher levels of social advancement and solutions for significant problems in crucial areas, exactly as Sam Altman designed it. A human-centered approach is essential for building foundational models, and decision-making must prioritize human behavior and emotion. Transparency and reliability are also critical, and the technology must operate in challenging environments with massive amounts of data, including edge computing.

Ultimately, human-centric AI will allow us to address the world's challenges from a more comprehensive perspective, rather than focusing on one application at a time. Our lives will become faster and more enriching, and we will learn more while solving more significant problems. This technology will be integrated into our daily lives and work.

In order to gauge progress in these areas, we must consider the advancements that will be made, such as solutions for weather and climate issues, mitigating job displacement, and reducing the prevalence of diseases globally. The outcomes of these efforts will serve as the primary metrics of success. It is essential to note that economic measures such as GDP are insufficient for evaluating the impact of AI on society. Instead, we must also consider the social impact, including the creation of new jobs, the preservation of existing ones, the emergence of novel and attractive fields, and the ability to combat diseases and climate change. These factors will serve as critical indicators of progress, indicating that we are moving in the right direction.

In order to make a difference, you must first comprehend the objectives of your action and the means by which you intend to accomplish them. If your efforts are unsuccessful, you can use this knowledge to identify alternative interventions. For example, if providing laptops to children for educational purposes[4] does not lead to increased learning due to lack of electricity or qualified teachers, then you can start designing new strategies and experiments.

Assessment Tools, Criteria, and KPIs to Better Understand Future R&D

Many companies are now moving beyond the traditional sales funnel and are seeking to understand customers in more holistic ways. This is evidenced by the 63%[5] of respondents who reported that they are using KPIs to develop a single, integrated view of the customer. To gain further insight into their customers, these companies are combining tactical KPIs into more strategic aggregates. Additionally, some interviewees have discussed their attempts to gain an understanding of "the customer journey," which covers all the points at which customers interact with brands today—as opposed to just focusing on the sales funnel.

Evolving Past Antiquated Metrics

Companies that are introducing AI must move beyond measuring maturity and adoption rates, instead focusing on creating a responsible and sustainable framework that emphasizes transparency, bias-free decision-making, and ethics.

AI has the potential to profoundly impact human norms, values, and society as a whole. It's crucial that we not only focus on ethics and optimization but also consider the broader implications of a human-centric future. To achieve this, we must define our long-term societal goals and prioritize a human-centric approach to AI that focuses on augmenting and enhancing our lives rather than just optimizing resources and reducing headcount.

In the past, AI platforms have primarily focused on optimizing resources and efficiency, but it's time to delve deeper and consider the emotional and sustainable impact of AI. A successful human-centric AI model should make us feel good and address our core needs as humans. We need to prioritize people as central to the AI process, involving them in managing, predicting, and building AI systems.

Furthermore, in this new human-centric, socially sustainable AI model, we need to consider sustainability as a critical factor. We can't just prioritize business interests; we must also take into account environmental, economic, and societal factors, as demonstrated by the growing importance of ESG (environmental, social, and governance) investing.

The Best AI for Good: Optimizing AI's Impact on Humanity

Artificial intelligence has the potential to make a significant impact on society and bring about groundbreaking innovations for humans in the future. This section answers questions about how to optimize AI's impact on humanity.

Which AI Use Case or Application Has the Biggest Positive Impact on Humanity?

Artificial intelligence has the potential to make a significant impact on society and bring about groundbreaking innovations for humans in the future. Its problem-solving capabilities could be used to tackle some of today's most pressing challenges, such as developing new drugs, reporting sexual harassment, combating human trafficking, optimizing renewable energy generation, and assisting people with disabilities. With proper utilization of AI, we can look forward to many more AI applications being developed for social good.[6]

An associate professor at a major university in Israel[7] has stated that AI will bring about many improvements in the next 12 years. These improvements are expected to be particularly beneficial in professions related to saving lives, such as individualized medicine and policing. AI will also allow for greater individualization of education, tailored to each student's needs and abilities. However, this could lead to increased unemployment in certain jobs that involve routine tasks, such as transportation drivers and food service.

How Can We Build High-Impact Organizations and Projects?

The advent of ChatGPT has elicited much excitement, particularly due to its potential impact on society. Its founder, Sam Altman, was driven by a desire to unearth and solve complex societal problems, including those related to renewable energy, disease control, and other daunting challenges. Altman's vision was always anchored on a human-centric approach, one that leverages the vast knowledge repositories of generative AI to enhance our quality of life.

In practical terms, this shift toward a more positive and AI-centric model is already taking place in smart cities. These cities are designed to provide better healthcare, infrastructure, mobility, and sustainable practices, all aimed at improving our overall quality of life. However, the success of this approach depends on getting the requirements right, which means shifting our conversations from the negative aspects of AI to the positive impact it can have on our lives.

The emergence of advanced technologies like ChatGPT and general AI presents us with opportunities to achieve unprecedented levels of innovation and break through to the next level of progress. Ultimately, the goal is to create a future in which we can spend more quality time with loved ones, live longer, and enjoy a better quality of life.

What AI Impact-Assessment Tools and Criteria Should We Use?

The use of AI has enabled businesses to innovate and operate differently; however, it is essential that organizations ensure that their governance practices are kept up-to-date alongside AI initiatives. Algorithmic Impact Assessments (AIAs) can be used to effectively manage the risks posed by AI systems. These assessments can be based on existing frameworks in data protection, privacy, and human rights policies, allowing organizations to build upon existing assessment processes. AIAs seek to achieve four main goals: capture an AI system's risk; cover full development life-cycle requirements; assess impact and increase accountability through a multi-stakeholder analysis; and facilitate go/no-go decisions. By conducting these assessments, organizations can gain insight into the potential benefits and risks of their AI systems as well as develop remediation processes for any identified issues.

Impact assessments are likely already familiar to your organization, so you can use these existing assessments as a foundation and build upon them when creating an AI-specific assessment. An AI assessment can provide important insights into the implications of artificial intelligence systems, while also helping you to effectively manage AI risks and ensure that responsible, ethical practices are in place. Remember that an AI assessment may represent an enhancement of existing processes rather than a completely new one.[8]

The Algorithmic Impact Assessment (AIA) is a mandatory risk assessment tool that supports Canada's Treasury Board's Directive on Automated Decision-Making. It is a questionnaire that helps identify the level of impact of an automated decision system. The AIA is composed of 48 risk and 33 mitigation questions that are used to calculate a score based on factors such as systems design, algorithm, decision type, impact, and data. This assessment follows Government of Canada policy and ethical and administrative law considerations for automated decision system risks that have been established through consultations with academia, civil society, and other public institutions.[9]

How Do We See the Feedback Loop and Aspects of Human-Centered Design?

The human-in-the-loop approach shifts the focus from simply "building a smarter system" to incorporating meaningful human interaction into the system. This approach is at the heart of research in interactive machine learning, which aims to create intelligent systems that can be controlled through human interaction. Examples of this type of research can be seen in works by Alison Parrish, an engineer, and at the Stanford HAI launch event in March 2019,[10] which showcased projects such as collaborative social systems, computers that learn to help, ambient intelligence in AI-assisted hospitals, and interaction design for autonomy. This concept is also known as "human-computer interaction."

Human-in-the-loop design strategies can often increase the efficiency of a system compared to fully automated and fully manual systems. This aligns with the idea that hybrid systems can perform at least as well as completely automated ones—that is, the human component can allow the rest of the system to take over when they choose—but with proper human interaction, it is possible to make the system better at its intended purpose. In other words, this is an optimal balance that results in superior performance.

How Do These Criteria Impact the Future of AI Research?

The impact of AI must not be solely disruptive. Instead, it should provide tangible benefits and value to society. This requires addressing the prerequisites of transparency, bias, and fairness, which are integral to creating a human-centric approach that transforms society. Failure to manage data properly, including issues of privacy and ethics, could lead to significant social implications. Visionaries such as Professor Geoffrey Hinton at the University of Toronto, Yann LeCun (VP and chief AI scientist at Meta), and Elon Musk are leading the charge in creating large-scale initiatives.

To create effective and ethical AI, the basics must be tackled first, including the creation of transparent, bias-free, and ethical systems. Once these fundamentals are established, AI can be harnessed to address significant societal issues such as healthcare, infrastructure, and education. This will require a long-term commitment to building a legacy through social AI that is human-centric and focused on value.

How Can Organizations and Institutions Come Together to Govern AI?

A majority of IT decision-makers believe that technologies powered by AI should be subject to regulation. Of those, 32% think this should come from a combination of government and industry, while 25% believe an independent industry consortium should take the lead.[11] Additionally, 94% feel that firms need to prioritize corporate responsibility and ethics when developing AI solutions. In order to ensure successful and sustainable AI regulation, businesses and governments must work together to create a governance framework that takes into account technology-enabled methods for managing inherent risks. This partnership will ensure that innovation, business growth, and trust in AI can all coexist harmoniously.

Expert Input and Analysis: Digital Transformation as a Business Transformation

by Nabil Nuaim, Senior Vice President of Digital & Information Technology at Saudi Aramco

Digital transformation is the integration of digital technology into all areas of a business, fundamentally changing how it operates and delivers value to customers, so in reality we see digital transformation as a business transformation. The idea is for the business to look at how it conducts itself and how it can leverage new digital technologies to drive company-wide operational performance improvements and benefits.

Painting a picture of the AI-powered future forces you to look at your assumptions on numerous possible future outcomes. These outcomes are influenced by personal beliefs that may bias the way we perceive the future. However, one would wish for a utopian future realized by these digital technologies—a future where famine is eliminated due to precision farming, where life expectancy is increased due to AI-powered disease prediction and precision medicine, and where AI productivity and efficiency gains will help spread economic prosperity.

Private enterprises and businesses must partner with all levels of government

To realize this utopian future, private enterprises and businesses must partner with all levels of government to drive change and agree what this change looks like. Digital transformation can help companies better meet their customers' expectations, improve operational efficiency, and leverage technology to their competitive advantage. But to achieve the win-win solution, it will require companies to integrate their approach to digital transformation into their overall business strategy, align their technology investments with their business goals, and most importantly acknowledge, openly and transparently, and address employee fears about the way jobs will change—and potentially be

(continued)

lost—while influencing these same employees to embrace these new digital technologies, harnessing their knowledge, skills, and capabilities to fully develop these digital initiatives for the benefit of everyone. In the same way that technology has transformed society before, digital transformation will undoubtedly be just as impactful. Ensuring that people are fully engaged with these technologies, that we incorporate programs to provide digital transformation-related education, and that we establish digital training institutes to deliver this digital future are some of the ways that private enterprises and businesses can partner with government to create policies and promote sustainability, innovation, and social responsibility during this transition. This in turn will lead to a more inclusive and equitable society where everyone benefits.

The Kingdom of Saudi Arabia commits to increase the percentage of electricity generation from renewable sources to reach 50% by 2030

Saudi Arabia's commitment to renewable energy is important for several reasons.

First, it shows that even a country with abundant fossil fuels can help drive a practical, stable, and inclusive energy transition, leveraging both conventional and alternative sources of energy with the aim of making overall energy more reliable, accessible, and sustainable. The role of oil in maintaining energy security during the transition is critical, and Aramco is well positioned due to our vast resources, and our low-cost, low upstream carbon-intensity operations. Second, the Kingdom's renewable energy strategy provides an example for other countries in the region that may be hesitant to invest in renewables. In terms of the goals, Saudi Arabia has tripled its renewable energy target and has successfully tendered for large-scale projects in wind and solar energy. Looking to the future, Saudi Arabia aims to generate 50% of its electricity from renewables by 2030. The country has also launched several initiatives to promote renewable energy, including the National Renewable Energy Program and the Saudi Green Initiative. While the path to achieving this commitment may not be easy, Saudi Arabia has already made significant progress toward its renewable energy goals and has the potential to become a leader in the transition to cleaner energy in collaboration with global partners.

AI plays an integral role in this push; the technology has the potential to increase renewable power generation and accurately forecast energy demand. AI can also introduce new, very efficient grid designs and plans, and optimize equipment operation, maintenance, and monitoring. Furthermore, AI can optimize the consumption and distribution of energy and support virtual power plants. Finally, AI excels at material discovery and synthesis to further disrupt the renewable industry.

How Do We Build Human Capacity and Talent?

It is essential to prioritize safety measures and ensure that the necessary precautions are taken prior to any potential accidents or incidents. Furthermore, there is a need to enhance the population's skill sets to keep up with technological advancements. While a portion of the population possesses digital and AI knowledge, a significant portion does not. Therefore, upskilling initiatives are crucial.

The importance of education cannot be overstated, beginning early in life and continuing throughout one's career. Companies need to recognize the significance of addressing these points as they embark on their AI journeys. Disrupting society is not the only aim; efficiency and optimization are important, but so is the impact on society as a whole.

It is crucial to ensure that the introduction of robotics and autonomous vehicles is done in a responsible and proactive manner, with consideration given to potential accidents and related issues. Additionally, the upskilling of the population is paramount. At present, a segment of society possesses digital knowledge, with an even smaller group possessing AI expertise. It is essential to bridge this knowledge gap via early education, continuing education in the workforce, and a commitment from companies to provide ongoing training.

What Do Humans Really Need from AI?

In order to build the future, it is important to deeply examine human needs. These include a desire for a good quality of life, longevity, family time, and ease of tasks. Additionally, we want to mature, grow, use our creativity, and develop a sustainability-driven approach. To accomplish this, collaborations or federations and ecosystem building are necessary, as noted by Shoshana Zuboff in her book *The Age of Surveillance Capitalism*.[12]

The focus must be on collaboration and ecosystem building, not competition or optimization. Positive impact, climate improvement, and reduced carbon emissions are necessary to create a more sustainable society. Resilience is also essential, as evidenced by the need to prepare for future pandemics. Industries, whether financial, manufacturing, or pharmaceutical, must prioritize stability and predictability in their supply chains and value chains. In order to achieve long-term goals, it is important to move away from short-term thinking and toward a more resilient perspective. The innovative technology of shared GPT should be viewed in this context.

12

The Future
I Envision
When I Dream

In March 2023, my mother passed away unexpectedly due to the collapse of the healthcare system in the United States. She suffered from negligence and did not receive the appropriate care based on her medical history and risk tolerance. This tragedy was exacerbated by the spread of a deadly fungus in hospitals.

My goal for the words you have read in this book is for them to help create a better future where people like my mother, a Holocaust survivor, can live longer and enjoy time with their loved ones—to create a future for my daughter, and everyone's children, that is sustainable and works for the betterment of all people.

However, the current state of the world deeply concerns me. We live in a polarized society that is divided on issues such as globalization and a shared vision for the future. This division may lead to two disconnected worlds, one led by the United States and its economic engine, and the other led by China with its unique philosophy and vision. It is impossible to predict the future with certainty, but by examining trends, we can gain some insight into how the world may look for future generations.

Education

In the coming years, technology will continue to advance rapidly, with significant developments in artificial intelligence (AI), robotics, biotech, and longevity. These technologies will play a much greater role in our lives than ever before.

As for work, there will be both job displacements and new job opportunities. The next generation will need to adapt to these changes and continually acquire new skills to remain competitive in the job market. Education will no longer be limited to traditional schooling but will include lifelong learning and the acquisition of skills from experience and emerging technologies.

Climate Science

Climate change is one of the most pressing environmental concerns of our time and will affect everyone, from children to seniors, with a greater impact on those in the Global South. Addressing climate change will require a concerted effort from individuals, companies, and governments worldwide.

My daughter's generation will play a crucial role in developing solutions to mitigate the impact of climate change and transition to a more sustainable way of living, using technologies like AI and possibly quantum computing. This will be especially important for those living in vulnerable areas like coastlines.

In the future, we must prioritize climate change and focus on both adaptation and mitigation efforts. The use of AI can enable the development of new climate models to predict extreme weather events and improve disaster preparedness and response. Such predictive models can have a significant impact on the mitigation of climate change and the development of better strategies to reduce the impact on vulnerable populations and ecosystems, especially in the Global South.

Carbon capture is another area that will receive significant attention. Recent innovations in carbon capture and storage have improved efficiency and cost-effectiveness, allowing industries to significantly reduce carbon emissions. AI will play a critical role in developing scalable carbon capture and storage solutions, helping us reach global emission reduction targets.

AI's data-driven approach will play a major role in environmental policy. Governments and organizations can leverage AI to make informed decisions on sustainability measures and develop more effective and targeted personalized policies.

I firmly believe that AI has the potential to revolutionize environmental policymaking by enabling data-driven decisions that benefit our planet and its inhabitants. The impact of AI on sustainable manufacturing and supply chain processes cannot be overstated, particularly in light of the supply chain disruptions caused by the COVID-19 pandemic. The optimization and automation tools made possible by AI will reduce waste, improve efficiency, and minimize environmental impact, leading to more sustainable production methods, digital twin technology, new digital factories, promoting a circular economy, and reducing the strain on natural resources such as water.

Diversity and Culture

Despite the current global divisions, we need to prioritize understanding and appreciating diversity and culture, and the younger generation will need to work together with people from different groups across the planet to achieve this.

Health

AI will also play a crucial role in healthcare, particularly in developing personalized medicine, treatment plans, disease eradication, and prevention strategies. By leveraging data-driven approaches, AI will help address staffing, resource, and process challenges, ultimately improving our longevity, quality of life, and overall balance. The potential for a sustainable future powered by AI is vast, and it is imperative that we capitalize on this potential to ensure a thriving planet for generations to come.

We need to make advances in medical technology to address issues like cancer and improve longevity. This will require a shift toward preventive care and personalized medicine, and my daughter's generation stands to benefit greatly from these developments, enjoying a longer and healthier life expectancy.

Social issues are increasingly becoming a focal point as society and priorities shift. It is my belief that the next generation, including my daughter, will possess the capability to shape the world around them, focusing on issues that hold significant meaning for them personally.

The areas of focus for this generation will revolve around social implications, with an emphasis on creating a sustainable planet, achieving equality, and upholding human and women's rights. However, it is important to note that the implementation of AI will be essential to addressing these issues effectively.

In order to use AI optimally, trust and control must be prioritized while improving the framework and tools used. Rather than focusing solely on efficiency and profiteering, AI must be used to drive positive change.

The Future of Remote Work

Work–life balance is another aspect that is predicted to shift dramatically. Continuous vacation and a commitment to life outside of work, as seen in some European countries, may become less distinct from dedicated work hours. The rise of remote work has already begun, with companies divided between bringing employees back to work in person and those advocating for continued remote work. This generation may redefine work–life balance, prioritizing well-being, flexibility, and mental health.

Space Exploration

Finally, advancements in space exploration are expected to continue, with the potential for interstellar travel. The next generation may witness significant developments in this area, including the exploration of human and nonhuman life beyond Earth's boundaries. It is conceivable that habitats may be set up in our solar system and beyond, although the exact nature of the future remains uncertain.

Commitment to Open Dialogue

My goal is to engage in a discussion about the technological advances that are being made, while also addressing the societal and social challenges that come along with them. Through this discussion, I hope to identify new models that can help make a positive impact on the planet.

In order to achieve this, I believe we need to establish the right framework, tools, skills, and values, such as resilience and adaptability, to navigate the changes and challenges that come with building a sustainable world powered by AI for the next generation. With these in place, I am confident that my daughter, and others of her generation, will be equipped to navigate the opportunities and challenges that lie ahead.

I am committed to advocating for the integration of AI in our social agenda, particularly as we enter a critical time where our planet's sustainability is at risk. The concept of Japanese Society 5.0 emphasizes the importance of prioritizing human beings and our planet, fostering resilience, inclusivity, and technological empowerment, including AI.

Moreover, AI will continue to play a critical role in education, particularly in promoting awareness of sustainability and environmental issues, and fostering a more environmentally conscious society. AI will also facilitate communication and collaboration across various industries and sectors, as exemplified by the Japanese Society 5.0 model, which emphasizes a holistic approach to improving the environment, healthcare, and the health of the planet.

AI has vast potential, and with proper implementation it can bring about significant benefits. In conclusion, I remain committed to advocating for critical areas of concern for our planet and humanity, including the establishment of a just, inclusive, and sustainable society.

Over the past decade, I have worked closely with international groups such as the World Economic Forum, G20, B20, the UN, and other councils, and I will continue to be involved in these efforts. I firmly believe that foundations such as the Good Foundation and other similar organizations are necessary to address crises, whether they be related to climate change or education.

I aim to identify and work with companies worldwide that can contribute to this mission and understand their unique challenges and dilemmas to find viable recommendations. Additionally, I hope to bring together groups of peers to build communities and engage in meaningful discussions about these issues.

As we strive to create a sustainable future, it is crucial to remember that we are not alone, and we must collaborate and fight for the preservation of our planet and humanity. We are fighting for our civilization, we're fighting for our humanity. And we cannot be absorbed by people who are focusing on just profits and greed and efficiency and optimization. There is another way, a better way.

Notes

Chapter 1

1. B.J. Copeland, "Artificial Intelligence (AI)," *Encyclopedia Britannica*, July 20, 1998, http://www.britannica.com/technology/artificial-intelligence.
2. Nick Srnicek, *Platform Capitalism* (John Wiley & Sons, 2017).
3. Martin Kenney and John Zysman, "The Rise of the Platform Economy," *Issues in Science and Technology* 32, no. 3 (March 1, 2016): 61–69, https://www.researchgate.net/publication/309483265_The_Rise_of_the_Platform_Economy.
4. K. Sabeel Rahman, *Democracy Against Domination* (Oxford University Press, 2017).
5. K. Sabeel Rahman and Kathleen Thelen, "The Rise of the Platform Business Model and the Transformation of Twenty-First-Century Capitalism," *Politics & Society* 47, no. 2 (March 22, 2019): 177–204, https://doi.org/10.1177/0032329219838932.
6. Pepper D. Culpepper and Kathleen Thelen, "Are We All Amazon Primed? Consumers and the Politics of Platform Power," *Comparative Political Studies* 53, no. 2 (June 11, 2019): 288–318, https://doi.org/10.1177/0010414019852687.
7. ITnation | L'actualité des professionnels de l'IT au Luxembourg, "Millennials and Generation Z: Shaping the Digital Workspace," accessed April 26, 2023, https://itnation.lu/news/millennials-and-generation-z-shaping-the-digital-workspace/.

8. H. James Wilson and Paul Daugherty, "How Humans and AI Are Working Together in 1,500 Companies," *Harvard Business Review*, July–August, 2018, https://hbr.org/2018/07/collaborative-intelligence-humans-and-ai-are-joining-forces.

9. Julien Boudet, Brian Gregg, Kathryn Rathje, Eli Stein, and Kai Vollhardt, "The Future of Personalization—and How to Get Ready for It," McKinsey & Company, June 18, 2019, http://www.mckinsey.com/capabilities/growth-marketing-and-sales/our-insights/the-future-of-personalization-and-how-to-get-ready-for-it.

10. Blake Morgan, "50 Stats Showing the Power of Personalization," *Forbes*, February 18, 2020. http://www.forbes.com/sites/blakemorgan/2020/02/18/50-stats-showing-the-power-of-personalization/.

11. Sam Daley, "36 Artificial Intelligence Examples Shaking Up Business Across Industries." *Built In*, August 9, 2021, https://builtin.com/artificial-intelligence/examples-ai-in-industry.

12. Ibid.

Chapter 2

1. Michael Chui, Martin Harrysson, James Manyika, Roger Roberts, Rita Chung, Pieter Nel, and Ashley van Heteren, "Applying Artificial Intelligence for Social Good," McKinsey & Company, November 28, 2018, http://www.mckinsey.com/featured-insights/artificial-intelligence/applying-artificial-intelligence-for-social-good.

2. George Hopkin, "AI and IoT Help Bring about a Smart City Experience," *Technology*, August 25, 2022, https://technologymagazine.com/ai-and-machine-learning/ai-and-iot-help-bring-about-a-smart-city-experience.

3. Electricity Maps, "Announcing Our Partnership with Google," blog post, April 23, 2020, http://www.electricitymaps.com/blog/announcing-our-partnership-with-google.

4. Bernard Marr, "10 Wonderful Examples of Using Artificial Intelligence (AI) for Good," *Forbes*, June 22, 2020, http://www.forbes.com/sites/bernardmarr/2020/06/22/10-wonderful-examples-of-using-artificial-intelligence-ai-for-good/.

5. Benjamin H. Kann, Reid Thompson, Charles R. Thomas, Adam Dicker, and Sanjay Aneja, "Artificial Intelligence in Oncology: Current Applications

and Future Directions," *Oncology* 33, no. 2 (February 15, 2019), http://www.cancernetwork.com/view/artificial-intelligence-oncology-current-applications-and-future-directions.

6. Marr, "10 Wonderful Examples."

7. Hamid Maher, Hubertus Meinecke, Damien Gromier, Mateo Garcia-Novelli, and Ruth Fortmann, "AI Is Essential for Solving the Climate Crisis," BCG Global, July 4, 2022, http://www.bcg.com/publications/2022/how-ai-can-help-climate-change.

8. Roberta Kwok, "AI Empowers Conservation Biology," *Nature* 567 (March 7, 2019): 133–134, http://www.nature.com/articles/d41586-019-00746-1.

9. AI for Sustainable Development Goals (AI4SDGs) Think Tank, "Nutrition Early Warning System (NEWS)," accessed April 26, 2023, http://www.ai-for-sdgs.academy/case/188.

10. ITU, "Artificial Intelligence for Good," January 2023, http://www.itu.int/en/mediacentre/backgrounders/Pages/artificial-intelligence-for-good.aspx.

11. AI Fairness 360 – Resources, "Welcome to AI Fairness 360," IBM Research Trusted AI, accessed April 26, 2023, http://aif360.mybluemix.net/resources.

12. Charlotte Edmond, "Here's How AI Is Helping Secure Water for Your Future," Microsoft On The Issues, October 22, 2019, https://news.microsoft.com/on-the-issues/2019/10/22/ai-water-scarcity-technology/.

13. Google, "Meet the Man on a Mission to Clean Up Africa's Air Using AI," accessed April 26, 2023, https://about.google/stories/clean-air-for-kampala/.

14. Krystal Vasquez, "How Artificial Intelligence Can Help Save Us from Air Pollution," *Environmental Health News*, August 12, 2021, http://www.ehn.org/air-pollution-artificial-intelligence-2654239069.html.

15. Jacques Bughin, Jeongmin Seong, James Manyika, Michael Chui, and Raoul Joshi, "Notes from the AI Frontier: Modeling the Impact of AI on the World Economy," McKinsey & Company, September 4, 2018, http://www.mckinsey.com/featured-insights/artificial-intelligence/notes-from-the-ai-frontier-modeling-the-impact-of-ai-on-the-world-economy#part2.

16. Michael Lokshin and Nithin Umapathi, "AI for Social Protection: Mind the People," Brookings, February 23, 2022, http://

www.brookings.edu/blog/future-development/2022/02/23/ai-for-social-protection-mind-the-people/.

Chapter 3

1. Theresa Agovino, "What Will the Workplace Look Like in 2025?," SHRM, August 18, 2021, https://www.shrm.org/hr-today/news/all-things-work/pages/the-workplace-in-2025.aspx.
2. Goldman Sachs, "Generative AI Could Raise Global GDP by 7%," April 5, 2023, https://www.goldmansachs.com/insights/pages/generative-ai-could-raise-global-gdp-by-7-percent.html.
3. Russell Pearlman, "The Return of the Gig Economy," *Briefings*, issue 57, December 6, 2022, https://www.kornferry.com/insights/briefings-magazine/issue-57/the-return-of-the-gig-economy.
4. Agovino, "What Will the Workplace Look Like in 2025?"
5. Vivian Giang, "What Will Work Look Like in 2030?" *Fast Company*, January 12, 2015, https://www.fastcompany.com/3040701/what-will-work-look-like-in-2030.
6. Pearlman, "The Return of the Gig Economy."
7. Ibid.
8. Agovino, "What Will the Workplace Look Like in 2025?"
9. Giang, "What Will Work Look Like In 2030?"
10. Robbert van Eerd and Jean Guo, "Jobs Will Be Very Different in 10 Years. Here's How to Prepare," World Economic Forum, January 17, 2020, https://www.weforum.org/agenda/2020/01/future-of-work/.
11. Agovino, "What Will the Workplace Look Like in 2025?"
12. van Eerd and Guo, "Jobs Will Be Very Different in 10 Years."
13. Hasan Bakhshi, Jonathan M. Downing, Michael A. Osborne, and Philippe Schneider, *The Future of Skills: Employment in 2030* (London: Pearson and Nesta, 2017), https://futureskills.pearson.com/research/assets/pdfs/technical-report.pdf.
14. McKinsey Global Institute, "Skill Shift: Automation and the Future of the Workforce," discussion paper, McKinsey & Company, May 2018, https://www.mckinsey.com/~/media/mckinsey/industries/public%20and%20social%20sector/our%20insights/skill%20shift%20automation%20and%20the%20future%20of%20the%20workforce/mgi-skill-shift-automation-and-future-of-the-workforce-may-2018.pdf.

15. Adam Jezard, "Who and What Is 'Civil Society'?," World Economic Forum, April 23, 2018, https://www.weforum.org/agenda/2018/04/what-is-civil-society/.
16. Bakhshi et al., *The Future of Skills*.
17. van Eerd and Guo, "Jobs Will Be Very Different in 10 Years."
18. Rohit Talwar, Steve Wells, Alexandra Whittington, April Koury, and Maria Romero, *The Future Reinvented: Reimagining Life, Society, and Business* (Fast Future Publishing, 2017).
19. James Manyika, Susan Lund, Michael Chui, Jacques Bughin, Jonathan Woetzel, Parul Batra, Ryan Ko, and Saurabh Sanghvi, "Jobs Lost, Jobs Gained: What the Future of Work Will Mean for Jobs, Skills, and Wages," McKinsey & Company, November 28, 2017, https://www.mckinsey.com/featured-insights/future-of-work/jobs-lost-jobs-gained-what-the-future-of-work-will-mean-for-jobs-skills-and-wages.
20. Charles McLellan, "Digital Transformation Is Changing. Here's What Comes Next," *ZDNET*, October 1, 2021, https://www.zdnet.com/article/digital-transformation-is-changing-heres-what-comes-next/.
21. OECD, "What Is the Future of Work?" accessed April 26, 2023, https://www.oecd.org/future-of-work/.
22. Ibid.

Chapter 4

1. Swetha Amaresan, "40 Customer Service Stats to Know in 2022," *HubSpot*, June 27, 2022, https://blog.hubspot.com/service/customer-service-stats.
2. Motista, "Leveraging the Value of Emotional Connection for Retailers," August 2019, https://inspirefire.com/wp-content/uploads/2019/08/3.3_Motista_Leveraging-Emotional-Connection-for-Retailers.pdf.
3. Michael Chui, James Manyika, and Mehdi Miremadi, "Four Fundamentals of Workplace Automation," McKinsey & Company, November 1, 2015, https://www.mckinsey.com/capabilities/mckinsey-digital/our-insights/four-fundamentals-of-workplace-automation.
4. NEOM, "Saudi Arabia's Plan to Build the Smartest City in the World," Bloomberg, April 28, 2021, https://sponsored.bloomberg.com/immersive/neom/smartest-city-in-the-world.

5. David Lee (David Kuo Chuen), Joseph Lim, Kok Fai Phoon, and Yu Wang, eds., "Fintech and Financial Inclusion," in *Foundations for Fintech* (World Scientific, 2022), 243–260, http://dx.doi.org/10.1142/9789811238819_0013.

Chapter 6

1. Samer Hassan and Primavera De Filippi, "The Expansion of Algorithmic Governance: From Code Is Law to Law Is Code," *Field Actions Science Reports: The Journal of Field Actions*, special issue 17: *Artificial Intelligence and Robotics in the City*, 2017.

Chapter 7

1. Gartner, "Gartner Says Nearly Half of CIOs Are Planning to Deploy Artificial Intelligence," press release, February 13, 2018, https://www.gartner.com/en/newsroom/press-releases/2018-02-13-gartner-says-nearly-half-of-cios-are-planning-to-deploy-artificial-intelligence.
2. McKinsey Analytics, "The State of AI in 2021," McKinsey & Company, December 2021, https://www.mckinsey.com/~/media/McKinsey/Business%20Functions/McKinsey%20Analytics/Our%20Insights/Global%20survey%20The%20state%20of%20AI%20in%202021/Global-survey-The-state-of-AI-in-2021.pdf.

Chapter 8

1. Mark Brayan, "What Companies Can Do to Build More Inclusive AI," World Economic Forum, September 30, 2021, https://www.weforum.org/agenda/2021/09/companies-how-to-build-more-inclusive-artificial-intelligence/.
2. Jennifer Langston, "Who's a CEO? Google Image Results Can Shift Gender Biases," *UW News*, April 9, 2015, https://www.washington.edu/news/2015/04/09/whos-a-ceo-google-image-results-can-shift-gender-biases/.
3. IBM Newsroom, "IBM Report: Cost of a Data Breach Hits Record High During Pandemic," July 28, 2021, https://newsroom.ibm.com/2021-07-28-IBM-Report-Cost-of-a-Data-Breach-Hits-Record-High--During-Pandemic.

4. Lance Whitney, "Data Privacy Is a Growing Concern for More Consumers," *TechRepublic*, August 17, 2021, https://www.techrepublic.com/article/data-privacy-is-a-growing-concern-for-more-consumers/.

Chapter 9

1. Emily A. Vogels, "Digital Divide Persists Even as Americans with Lower Incomes Make Gains in Tech Adoption," Pew Research Center, June 22, 2021, https://www.pewresearch.org/short-reads/2021/06/22/digital-divide-persists-even-as-americans-with-lower-incomes-make-gains-in-tech-adoption/.
2. Ariella Lehrer, "Games at Retail Are Definitely NOT Dying," blog post, September 7, 2021, https://ariellalehrer.com/games-at-retail-are-definitely-not-dying/.
3. Paul Griffin, "The Carbon Majors Database: CDP Carbon Majors Report 2017," CDP, July 2017, https://cdn.cdp.net/cdp-production/cms/reports/documents/000/002/327/original/Carbon-Majors-Report-2017.pdf?1501833772.

Chapter 10

1. Bergur Thormundsson, "Global Smart City Revenue 2020–2028," Statista, April 27, 2023, http://www.statista.com/statistics/1111626/worldwide-smart-city-market-revenue/.
2. Smart Waste Bin, "Bin-e," accessed April 26, 2023, http://www.bine.world/.
3. Tan Yigitcanlar et al., "Artificial Intelligence Technologies and Related Urban Planning and Development Concepts: How Are They Perceived and Utilized in Australia?" *Journal of Open Innovation: Technology, Market, and Complexity* 6, no. 4 (2020): 1–21, http://www.econstor.eu/bitstream/10419/241573/1/1744671109.pdf.
4. World Bank, "Urban Development," accessed April 26, 2023, http://www.worldbank.org/en/topic/urbandevelopment/overview.
5. Annie Brown, "Developing Coherent AI Infrastructure for Smart Cities," *Forbes*, August 4, 2021, http://www.forbes.com/sites/anniebrown/2021/08/04/developing-coherent-ai-infrastructure-for-smart-cities/?sh=119a560e1d3f.

6. Deloitte, "City Operations Through AI," accessed April 26, 2023, http://www.deloitte.com/global/en/Industries/government-public/perspectives/urban-future-with-a-purpose/city-operations-throuh-ai.html.

7. Indian Prime Minister Narendra Modi launched the MyGov website, which has played a crucial role in leveraging artificial intelligence to combat the COVID-19 pandemic.

   The website incorporated an AI-enabled chatbot, known as MyGov Corona Helpdesk, to provide timely updates and essential information to citizens regarding COVID-19 https://www.mygov.in/simple-page/wall-mygov-champions/https://www.entrepreneur.com/en-in/technology/ways-in-which-artificial-intelligence-will-empower-business/372324

Chapter 11

1. Saif Malhem, Nupur Ruchika Kohli, and Lorny Pfeifer, "3 Ways Global Youth Is Securing Responsible AI." World Economic Forum, October 5, 2022, http://www.weforum.org/agenda/2022/10/how-the-global-youth-is-securing-responsible-ai/.

2. United Nations Development Programme, "Global Youngsters Put Forward Innovative AI Solutions for SDGs at the U&AI Youth Bootcamp Final," November 22, 2021, http://www.undp.org/china/press-releases/global-youngsters-put-forward-innovative-ai-solutions-sdgs-uai-youth-bootcamp-final.

3. Intel, "AI for Youth Uses Intel Technology to Solve Real-World Problems," June 25, 2020, http://www.intel.com/content/www/us/en/newsroom/news/ai-youth-intel-technology-solve-real-problems.html#gs.j6gfxj.

4. Andrew Dillon, "How to Measure Your Organization's Social Impact," Kellogg Insight, June 10, 2022, https://insight.kellogg.northwestern.edu/article/measure-your-organizations-social-impact.

5. Michael Schrage and David Kiron, "Leading with Next-Generation Key Performance Indicators," *MIT Sloan Management Review*, June 26, 2018, https://sloanreview.mit.edu/projects/leading-with-next-generation-key-performance-indicators/.

6. Ashish Sukhadeve, "Artificial Intelligence for Good: How AI Is Helping Humanity," *Forbes*, February 9, 2021, http://www.forbes.com/sites/forbesbusinesscouncil/2021/02/09/artificial-intelligence-for-good-how-ai-is-helping-humanity/.

7. Janna Anderson and Lee Rainie, "3. Improvements Ahead: How Humans and AI Might Evolve Together in the Next Decade," Pew Research Center, December 10, 2018, http://www.pewresearch.org/internet/2018/12/10/improvements-ahead-how-humans-and-ai-might-evolve-together-in-the-next-decade/.

8. Ilana Golbin, "Mitigate AI Risks with the Use of an Algorithmic Impact Assessment," PwC, October 28, 2021, http://www.pwc.com/us/en/tech-effect/ai-analytics/algorithmic-impact-assessments.html.

9. Government of Canada, "Algorithmic Impact Assessment Tool," accessed April 26, 2023, http://www.canada.ca/en/government/system/digital-government/digital-government-innovations/responsible-use-ai/algorithmic-impact-assessment.html.

10. Ge Wang, "Humans in the Loop: The Design of Interactive AI Systems," Stanford University Human-Centered Artificial Intelligence, October 20, 2019, https://hai.stanford.edu/news/humans-loop-design-interactive-ai-systems.

11. KPMG International, "The Shape of AI Governance to Come," January 2021, https://assets.kpmg.com/content/dam/kpmg/xx/pdf/2021/01/the-shape-of-ai-governance-to-come.pdf.

12. Shoshana Zuboff, *The Age of Surveillance Capitalism: The Fight for a Human Future at the New Frontier of Power* (PublicAffairs, 2019).

List of Contributors

Thank you to all who shared their wisdom with me to create this book.

Contributor	Title of Expert Analysis	Location
Sylvain Duranton, Global Leader of BCG X, and Senior Partner and Managing Director of Boston Consulting Group	Work at BCG Is Responsibility and Contribution to the Betterment of Society	Chapter 2
Laurent Guengant, Vice President—Global Environmental Business Division—Head of EMEA Corporate Venture—at Hitachi	Hitachi to Positively Impact Climate Change Through Its Investments, Market Presence, and Initiatives	Chapter 2
Dr. Sokwoo Rhee, Corporate Senior Vice President at LG Electronics and Head of the LG North America Innovation Center	How LG Is Improving Quality of Life Through Innovation	Chapter 2
James Hodson, Chief Executive Officer of AI for Good Foundation Blueprint for an AI-Enabled Society	AI and Social Contract Perspective	Chapter 3

(*continued*)

Contributor	Title of Expert Analysis	Location
Tiger Tyagarajan, President and Chief Executive Officer of Genpact	How Genpact Leverages Technology for Critical Challenges to Humanity	Chapter 3
Sylvain Duranton, Global Leader of BCG X, and Senior Partner and Managing Director of Boston Consulting Group	AI: The Most Digital Disruptive Transformation Model That Will Benefit Humankind	Chapter 4
Atti Riazi, Senior Vice President and Chief Information Officer, Hearst Corporation	As We Embrace AI, We Must Ensure We Fully Understand the Ethical Questions It Poses	Chapter 4
Katia Walsh, PhD, award-winning global technology, data, and AI cross-industry leader; Fortune 500 board director; pioneer of digital upskilling and responsible AI	Applications of Data and AI at Scale to Reimagine the Future with a Focus on Sustainability	Chapter 4
Alan Boehme, former Chief Technology Officer at H&M Group, Procter & Gamble, and Coca-Cola	Reimagining the Future of the Industry with a Focus on Sustainability	Chapter 4
Tsvi Gal, Head of Enterprise Technology Services (Infrastructure) at Memorial Sloan Kettering Cancer Center	Future of Self-Improving AI and Artificial Neural Networks	Chapter 5
Vincenzo Aquaro, Chief of Digital Government Branch—Division for Public Institutions and Digital Government—DESA—United Nations	How AI Is Positively and Negatively Impacting SDGs	Chapter 6

Contributor	Title of Expert Analysis	Location
Kay Firth-Butterfield, Executive Director, Centre for Trustworthy Technology, a World Economic Forum Centre for the Fourth Industrial Revolution, former Head of Artificial Intelligence and a member of the Executive Committee of the World Economic Forum	AI Helps Both Business and Governments Model for a More Resilient Future	Chapter 6
Robert Opp, Chief Digital Officer, UNDP	Sustainable Development Goals and the Greatest Existential Risks That Humanity Face	Chapter 6
Stephen Ibaraki, Chairman of REDDS Capital, Microsoft 20 Global Awards with 2018–2023 MVP in AI, investor/venture capitalist, futurist, Founder and Chair of Outreach of UN ITU AI for Good Global Summit	What Human–Machine Interaction Should Be	Chapter 8
Toshie Takahashi, AI for Good; Youth and AI/Robots; Professor of Waseda University, Tokyo; Associate Fellow of the CFI at the University of Cambridge	What Young People Are Saying	Chapter 11
Nabil Nuaim, Senior Vice President of Digital & Information Technology at Saudi Aramco	Digital Transformation as a Business Transformation	Chapter 11

Acknowledgments

I'm thankful for the exceptional help and contributions of my close friend and colleague, William Saulsbery, who served as the lead content project manager for this massive book project. With his professional support and orchestration, we managed the content flow and coordinated overall efforts, including marketing. Despite the continuously changing book schedule, he ensured that we stayed on track.

I want to express my gratitude to Angelica Sirotin, my dear friend and colleague, for her hard work and valuable strategic ideas. Despite her busy schedule, she prioritized contributing her best efforts, which played a significant role in the project's success. Angelica is an exceptional talent, and I am grateful for her unwavering commitment to making a positive impact, no matter what it takes. I would like to express my gratitude to Sandra Loppe Bello for generously assisting with the administrative and logistical aspects of this book and Adi Gal for her dedicated contributions to multiple research aspects of this book while she was studying abroad at University. Without their help, this book would not have been possible.

I am deeply grateful to the many colleagues who contributed their great ideas to this book and to all those who have taught me about sustainability, climate, social impact, and artificial intelligence over the years.

I want to express my special thanks and gratitude to Eddie Trump, a dear friend who went beyond expectations to help me during the most challenging time of my life. When COVID-19 struck me in Miami, Eddie played a crucial role in saving my life.

I also want to express my deepest thanks and gratitude to my many dear friends and mentors around the world. I am grateful for their unwavering support, belief, and guidance, which has been an invaluable source of motivation during difficult times.

I am grateful to my parents for giving me the opportunity and drive to pursue the American Dream. One should never underestimate the power of perseverance, grit, and resilience. Unfortunately, my mother passed away while I was in the process of writing this book. It is a significant loss and profoundly saddens me, but her memory will live forever with me.

I want to express my sincere gratitude to my wife, Susanna, for always keeping me grounded and motivating me to push beyond my limits, especially during challenging times. She supports my creative ideas and patiently endures my highs and lows as I strive to make a positive impact on our planet. Thank you, Susanna, for everything.

I want to express my deep appreciation to my daughter, Becky, who constantly introduces me to fresh perspectives and innovative ideas in our ever-changing digital world. Your vibrant imagination is a treasure that I hope you will keep for the rest of your life. Your presence in our lives has brought us immense joy and happiness, and we are truly grateful for you. We believe that you will achieve great things and make a positive impact on the world. With over 1.1 billion girls under the age of 18, you are part of a generation of women who are set to become the largest group of female leaders, entrepreneurs, and change-makers the world has ever seen. Remember, little girls with big dreams become women of purpose, and you are one of those amazing girls who have the potential to change the world.

About the Author

Mark Minevich is a highly regarded and trusted digital cognitive AI strategist, artificial intelligence expert, global social innovation and technology executive, UN advisor, leading author and columnist, private investor/venture capitalist, and the principal founder and president of Going Global Ventures.

Mark is co-chair of the steering committee of the AI for the Planet Alliance in collaboration with UNDP, UNESCO, and Boston Consulting Group (BCG) as a knowledge partner based in Paris. Mark is currently a UN advisor/consultant to UNDESA—United Nations Department of Economic and Social Affairs—focusing on digital government.

Mark is a Chairman of the executive committee of AI for Good Foundation.

Mark is a founding partner and chairman of Going Global Ventures (GGV), a New York-based investment, technology, and strategic advisory firm dedicated to leading high-growth tech clients to success in the global digital economy. GGV advises large global enterprises and brands in the United States, the European Union, South America, and Japan and collaborates with leading investment organizations and private wealth focused on digitalization and artificial intelligence.

Mark is senior advisor to Boston Consulting Group and BCG Gamma. Currently, he serves as the strategic advisor and global ambassador to the CEO and chairman of New York-based Amelia/IPsoft Inc.

Mark collaborates and advises large global enterprises both in the United States and Japan. In Japan, he advises Hitachi on disruptive technology, AI, and climate change. He is also on advisory board to AI Lab, Josef Stefan Institute, Saudi Data and Artificial Intelligence Authority (SDAIA) and Institute for Artificial Intelligence of Serbia.

Mark is a private investor and is a business advisor to Infosec Global and DarwinAI, among others. He was an early member of founding management teams for successful startups that attracted investment and created exits such as ClubMom, VitaSave, and others. Mark also advises several venture capital and investment companies. Mark is a Special Advisor for BootstrapLabs– a pioneer in the realm of VC funds focused on applied AI and advisory partner to Canadian Growth Investments.

Mark was appointed as a member of World Economic Forum Future Council and is involved with WEF initiatives.

Mark was a member of the B20 with the G20 under the presidency of Indonesia and has been a leading member of the B20 digitalization task forces since 2016. Mark has served as a member of the B20 with the G20 during the Germany, Argentina, Japan, Saudi Arabia, Italy, Indonesia presidency.

Mark is a senior fellow of the Council on Competitiveness in Washington, DC, and senior fellow of the Global Federation of Competitiveness Councils. Mark is the co-founder and founding chair of the Digital Pioneers Network and the AI Pioneers Circle, based in New York.

Mark has significant experience in venture capital and private equity. He has served as venture advisor to Global Emerging Markets, an alternative investment group that manages a diverse set of investment vehicles, carrying with it a mature fund and portfolio of 24 applied AI companies.

Prior to this position, Mark was the vice chair of Ventures and External Affairs, as well as CTO at the Comtrade Group, an international technology conglomerate. He also served as the CTO and strategy executive at IBM, and held other management, technology, and strategy roles that entailed formulating investment tactics for venture capital incubation programs.

Mark was also involved with Research Board, a Gartner company and international think tank advising CIOs at some of the world's largest corporations, such as Deutsche Bank, the BTM Corporation, Geotek Communications, Qwest Communications, Comcast, and USWEB/CKS.

Mark is also involved in media and journalism, and contributes to a number of publications, including *Fast Company, Forbes, VentureBeat, WEF, Entrepreneur, Observer, TechCrunch, InformationWeek, CIO Magazine,* and *Cognitive World.* His work has been cited and featured in articles and has appeared in *Newsweek, Inc., CIO Magazine, Hitachi Review/Japan, Telegraph UK,* CNBC, and other influential media outlets. Mark is a respected voice in the tech innovation community. His knowledge has been cited and his name has been featured in articles on an international scale.

Mark was named one of the 20 AI Influencers and Visionaries for 2021 and 2022. *Forbes* named Mark one of the Leaders to Watch in 2017. He has received the Albert Einstein Award for Outstanding Achievement and the World Trade Leadership Award from the World Trade Centers and World Trade Center's Association.

Index

213